Bread in our Hands

Bread in our Hands

Feeding God's People in Hungry Times

Julie M. Hulme

Cover image © PureStockX

Scripture quotations are from the New Revised Standard Version of the Bible (Anglicized Edition), © 1989, 1995 by the Division of Christian Education of the National Council of the Churches of Christ in the United States of America. Used by permission. All rights reserved.

British Library Cataloguing in Publication data
A catalogue record for this book is available
from the British Library

ISBN 978-1-905958-19-1

First published by Inspire
4 John Wesley Road
Werrington
Peterborough PE4 6ZP

Printed and bound in Great Britain by
Printondemand-worldwide.com, Peterborough

Acknowledgements

I wish to express my most profound gratitude to the Sisters of the Love of God at the Convent of the Incarnation, Fairacres, Oxford, who – through their hospitality, publications, example and wise guidance over the past three decades – have shown me what prayer can be. They, along with members of my family, our support group, and many other friends and colleagues, have nourished me with their patient, persistent, prayerful loving.

Over the years I have had some outstanding teachers: at Durham University; Wesley College, Bristol; Wesley House and its partner institutes in Cambridge; and latterly, colleagues in the Birmingham District, especially those connected with the Queens Foundation. If I have learned anything about the Bible, it is due to them. Any errors of interpretation or unwarranted speculations are entirely my own.

Of all my teachers, the Revd Bill Denning probably made the most impact in the shortest time. I attended a couple of his workshops on creativity during the late 1980s and visited him, briefly, at Maypole Farm, Thornbury, during the same period. In his ability to help ordinary people to explore the Bible and their own spirituality, Bill was an inspiration, a true artist, and far ahead of his time. I am just one of the many hundreds of people that he helped to pray using paint and clay.

I am indebted to all those who have believed in me, encouraged me, exhorted me and, at times, admonished me, over the past five years, as I have tested and refined these ideas in sermons, synods, addresses, articles, meetings, workshops, retreats and quiet days. When I get excited by my material, the effect can be rather like that of a steamroller heading downhill, but it is never my intention to flatten anyone, and so I would like to say a particular 'thank you' to those who have disagreed with me, and to assure you that all the feedback has been useful, even when unexpected and, occasionally, unwelcome.

Much of this work has been done amongst women, and I am particularly grateful to the Women's Network of the Methodist Church, especially the Resource Team of the Birmingham District, with whom I have shared an experience of 'thinking differently' during a period of profound change for the movement. A small group of 'wise men' – David Bagwell, Tim Crome, David Vonberg and David Wetton – read parts of the book as it was being written, providing other perspectives and some very valuable comments. At mph, Natalie Watson commissioned the work, and Susan Hibbins saw it through to publication: their encouragement, diligence and care have been most welcome.

Last, but not least, I could not have completed the book without the sustained and loving support of my husband, David, and our daughters, Cate and Debbie. Whatever else has been going on in our lives, they have always found the grace to believe in me. Knowing that, I have been able to do what has often seemed (to me, at least) to be impossible. This book is dedicated to them, with all my love, always.

Julie M. Hulme
February 2008

Contents

Acknowledgements

Introduction
A Place to Begin

During the afternoon of Friday, 20 July 2007, I stood for a few minutes on the surface of the Athabasca Glacier, one arm of the Columbia Icefield in the Canadian Rockies. Thousands of metres of snow had been compressed over tens of centuries to form the ice beneath my feet. The surface was puddled and slippery; streaked grey-brown where it carried dirt; turquoise where the air had been pressed out of the compacted snow.

As I stared at the ice-fall cresting the cliff before me, I felt as though I had travelled – in time and in space – to the source of life. I had seen valleys shaped by glaciers before, but here that power was still at work. I could see the ice for myself, touch it, feel its cold as near-frozen water soaked into my shoes. Snow-melt from the mountains above me fed rivers flowing west to the Pacific, north to the Arctic and east to the Atlantic oceans: rivers which embraced a vast continent, irrigating fields, carrying goods to market, satisfying the thirst of millions, providing a habitat for human beings, mammals, reptiles, fish, birds.

Here was a place linked to the world I knew, but at an almost unimaginable distance. It was so wholly other – bare rock, blown dust, chill wind and white glare, a cold empty brightness – like a blank page on which a world waited to be written: the world as it has come to be. The thought was a little frightening, but at the same time, it filled me. It felt like an encounter with an awesome, primeval force that still possessed the most immense potential. It was as though I had ventured into the ancient heart of the world and heard a pulse on the utmost edge of silence.

Sometimes you have to go to the margins in order to find the centre; wander off the track to rediscover where you want to go; set aside all you have learned so that you can regain the freshness, the vitality and the truth of what you already know. This was one of those moments. I was a long way from everything that was familiar, in a landscape where I would not survive for a day without specialized support. In another sense, standing on the glacier helped me to see what I knew already. We have to find our way to the Source of life: to the All that feeds us, and gives us the energy we need to be creative. And doing so is like coming home.

This is a book about what it means to be life-giving, and what it takes to remain so. It is a book about faith, hope and love; how the task of remaining faithful, hopeful and loving requires us to go deeper into prayer and, as we do so, to learn more about ourselves, as well as more about God. It is the Spirit which sows the seeds of love and truth within us, but there is a long, patient work to be done between sowing and reaping, and we are invited to collaborate with it. This is the 'work' of prayer, allowing the seeds to grow, blossom, fruit and reproduce themselves. No one else can do this work for you, but I hope this book will help you accomplish whatever it is you need to do.

Like any work, these pages emerge from a particular context and are 'written back' into it; and the context has many layers. At its broadest, there are the problems faced by all humanity in the twenty-first century: for example, the crisis in our relationship with the natural world. I was awed by my visit to the Athabasca Glacier, but the truth is that, due to climate change, the ice is disappearing. Photographs show how far the glaciers of the Canadian Rockies have retreated over the past hundred years or so. In my daughters' lifetimes, some may vanish altogether.

Creating a sustainable environment was just one of eight Millennium Development Goals agreed by heads of state and national governments at a United Nations' summit held in 2000. The others are equally necessary, urgent and ambitious: the eradication of extreme poverty and hunger; the provision of universal primary education; the promotion of gender equality and the empowerment of women; a reduction in child mortality and improvements to maternal health; work to combat HIV and AIDS, malaria and other diseases; and the development of global partnerships to pursue all these goals and more.

As we make progress on these issues, we will create a greater degree of justice in our international relationships and reduce the tensions which deteriorate into conflict, violence, war and genocide. To address issues of this size and complexity, however, will require all the energy, creativity and commitment we can muster. The forces of resistance are powerful, and we cannot solve these problems simply by throwing money or technology at them, nor will we find solutions by means of intellect alone. The sheer scale of the work will require vast amounts of compassion, honesty, generosity and trust.

These are spiritual resources, which we will have to find in the midst of all our other, everyday activities and despite the huge scale of the task. They are gifts from God, but we must learn to receive them if we wish to be more faithful, prayerful and creative. For it is only by knowing how to forgive and hope and endure that we will be able to keep on working for the common good. We will need emotional, psychological and spiritual strength to work alone; or against the current; or with difficult colleagues; or in unrewarding situations; persevering beyond any common sense.

The global issues of our time require an individual response, from people like us: people who will act with compassion and generosity, not because we are better than others (we are not) but because we love life, we accept that we are human, we want to live life to the full, and we want every other human being to enjoy an abundant life as well.

But how can we find the necessary resourcefulness, creativity and resilience? How can we find life enough to address the task? How can we love and pray and labour and trust – and go on doing so?

Every day we decide how to use our time, energy, talents and experience. Every day we face the challenge of investing these personal assets so that they will make a positive difference to the world. This is a spiritual struggle as well as a pragmatic endeavour. What can I do? Do I have something to offer here, and do I feel able to offer it? How can I make a generous response when I feel I have little to give?

We approach such questions with a ragbag of experience. Mine has included writing fiction, poems, reportage and prayers; a call to live the Ministry of Word and Sacrament as a life of prayer; an ongoing experiment with marriage and motherhood; pastoral leadership of congregations and in various other contexts within the Methodist Church; leading retreats and conferences; taking up art in my forties; depression, breast cancer, various forms of grief and, latterly, the long, tangled struggle to order my thoughts sufficiently to write this book.

We can each make our own list, but how do we work with our personal assortment to make the most generous response possible to the challenge of the times? Do we feel free to do this? To what extent do we accept limits on who we are and what we can do? Can we ever transcend them, and reach toward what we long to see?

Our ability to be creative rests on the level of our confidence, our sense of assurance, the depth of our conviction and our ability to trust. In other words, it depends on our ability to have faith, to grow in faith, to express that faith and to keep faith with those principles and persons – which may include God – in whom we believe. This, in turn, depends on how we see ourselves, others, life, the world and our place in it: above all, on how we see the resources available, both within us and around us.

Do we see ourselves as having the resources we need? If we do, we will feel resourced and resourceful. We will have the confidence to do whatever needs to be done. We will have faith in ourselves, in others, in life, and perhaps also in God. We will know that, if necessary, we have the confidence to act in faith, the courage to keep faith, and the compassion to step out in faith. We will have the flexibility, generosity and resilience to be imaginative – whatever happens – and to persevere as long as is necessary.

Do we see ourselves as having the resources we need? The question applies, whether we are thinking as individuals, congregations, communities or nations. It applies whatever the scale of the challenge before us. This is why the matter of faith is critical to the Church in Britain as it faces a diminishment in size, strength and social influence. In many parts of the Church, there is a severe shortage of people, money, energy and ideas. So much of what we do no longer nourishes us, or can no longer be sustained. This depletion of resources has undermined our faith in ourselves, in one another and in God. Grief and anxiety are persistent and pervasive. They wear us down and wear us out.

How do we withstand this attrition? Only by putting ourselves in the way of replenishment. What if we are not sure how to do this? What if we do not know how we are 'fed', or the resources which normally feed us are no longer available, or if nothing seems to be 'enough' for our need?

What we need is an input of whatever it is that will build up our faith. We need feeding. We need the bread of life, renewal, an infilling of the Holy Spirit, the 'more life' or abundant life that God has promised to give us. There are many ways to describe this 'input' but we know it by the way it enlarges our vision and empowers us to try new things – or enables us to keep on doing the same things as before, but with fresh enthusiasm, commitment and purpose.

So often we are exhorted to 'have faith' as if it is obvious what faith is and how we acquire it. But we have to learn how to find the life we need, not only from the Scriptures, but from our experience and our interaction with others. If we know how we are fed, we will know how to identify the food which encourages, equips and enables us; whatever we need, whenever we need it, as often as we need it. We will find our way to the source of life.

The good news is that this is what Jesus of Nazareth shows us. He teaches us how to have faith. And in the feeding of the five thousand – a situation where the resources are scarce but the need is enormous – he demonstrates how we can apply faith, step by step, so that everyone is satisfied, and God's promised feast is made real.

His 'way' of faith is a process with two elements: a specific vision of the life God gives; and a strategy for conveying, creating or magnifying that life. The gospel is good news because this process is the way in which the abundant life of God becomes a shared experience of living life to the full.

In *Bread in Our Hands: Feeding God's People in Hungry Times* the 'bread in our hands' is twofold: the resources which are available, within us and around us; and the 'way' of faith which Jesus teaches, which shows us what to do with what we have 'in our hands'. It is this 'way' which I have sought to 'unpack' a little in this book. It will soon become clear that I have barely begun to scratch the surface of all that can be said.

Although I am writing about who we are and how we respond to the world around us, I assume that we are not only concerned about ourselves. We ask 'How am I fed?', not only for our own benefit, but because we are involved in 'feeding' others. So although this book has a deliberate 'inward' focus, I am taking it for granted that we look inward in order to then look outward in ever-increasing circles. I have avoided defining what the 'mission' is, because it depends on the context; but I assume that it is always love.

Similarly, I have avoided defining who the 'others' might be because I don't think it matters. They can be your family and friends, your neighbours or colleagues. They can be strangers, even enemies. Members of your team, house-group or congregation, or of another group or society that you are trying to understand. People in another country whose troubles are highlighted by the news of the day. In the end, they are all 'God's people', because God loves them all.

I have not explained in detail why these are 'hungry times'. In many ways and for many people, of course, they are not obviously so. The image is useful, however, because I want to concentrate on those situations where the abundant life that God gives is not seen, and begin to address the question of how we can collaborate with the Spirit to realize God's vision there.

Please feel free to read this book in the way which suits you. Each chapter consists of a piece of creative writing, followed by six prose pieces; each of which is followed by questions, a suggested Bible passage, and a reflection. In a few sections, the questions are embedded in the text. The arrangement allows you to read the book as a connected argument, or use it as an aid to thematic Bible study, self-examination, journal-writing and prayer.

The themes can be supported by material from almost anywhere in the Bible, but for the purposes of this book I have confined myself to commenting on one version of the feeding of the five thousand, that given by Mark (6.30–44), so that I can show how the issues raised by the story underpin the gospel/Gospel as a whole. I chose Mark because most scholars believe it was the first to be written. It is also the shortest of the four, but even so, I found that to keep the material manageable it was necessary to avoid referring to other parts of the New Testament. I encourage you to make your own connections. The Bible passages suggested for further reflection are all from the Old Testament because I want to suggest that the gospel of abundant life is fundamental to our understanding of the Hebrew scriptures. That is where John the Baptist and Jesus of Nazareth found it, before making it their own. I hope that the following summary and outline will help you find your way through the book.

Broadly speaking, Chapter 1 addresses Jesus' teaching as a process or 'way' of faith. This 'way' consists of two elements: a vision of God's life as abundant in every possible sense, and a strategy whereby this abundance is made personal, practical, specific and real. Chapters 2 and 3 explore the significance of Jesus' vision, focusing particularly on the image of the Feast of the kingdom. Chapters 4–7 examine the strategy which, step by step, makes the vision into a reality. We receive what is given, even though it is not enough. We give thanks, even though it is not enough. We act as if it is enough to meet the need. And we persist in acceptance, gratitude and 'acting as if' until the resources have become enough to meet the need.

In Chapter 1, 'A Way to Feed the Multitude', we look at Jesus' attitude to mission through his instruction to the Twelve that they are to 'travel light'. They are able to do this because the 'one thing' he does encourage them to take is their specialized knowledge of faith as the tool which will enable them to find all the other resources they need.

In Chapter 2, 'The Prospect of a Feast', we reflect on the scope of Jesus' teaching, and in particular on the gospel as a story which shows us the life God wants us to receive. This is good news, providing we are able to see it. Jesus used images, such as the feast of the kingdom, to show people that God's promise of abundant life could be realized through following his 'way' of faith, confidence and trust.

In Chapter 3, 'Meeting the Multitude', we consider the impact of Jesus' teaching, his ability to 'deliver' and the fact that he taught his disciples to do the same. Jesus' 'way' of faith is the means whereby we find grace in the wilderness. But when the disciples met the multitude, their ability to help them was undermined by their own 'hunger'. How could they meet Jesus' challenge to feed the crowd?

In Chapter 4, 'Receiving the Gift', we begin to reflect on the strategy Jesus used to make his vision of abundant life real. The first step is to receive what is 'given', even though it is not enough for what we need to do. This is the gesture of acceptance, which creates a space in which change becomes possible. Acceptance includes our willingness to receive the 'child' and childlike qualities in ourselves, such as the ability to live in the 'now', and see the potential in what we hold.

In Chapter 5, 'The Art of Abundance', we explore the gesture of gratitude, through reflecting on what it may have meant for Jesus to offer a blessing, or give thanks over the food. We give thanks to God who has brought us to this moment, and given us resources to work with. This way of praying invites us to acknowledge the truth of God and the truth of ourselves, always and everywhere; to leave the essential contradiction between good and evil unresolved; but to choose to see life, potential and abundance.

In Chapter 6, 'The Way of Jesus', we examine how Jesus remained faithful to his vision of the feast, acting as if the bread in his hands was enough to feed the crowd and make the feast real. This is the gesture of commitment, in which he departs from the way that people normally behave and takes another road, continuing to 'act as if' the resources are enough, so that the extremes of God's abundant life and human hunger can meet. Following him, we apply our resources to the task before us, acting as if the vision of God's abundance is true, and acting as if the resources given are enough to meet the need. This requires us to 'step out into the air' and take small, even symbolic, steps, trusting in the process which allows extremes to meet.

Finally, in Chapter 7, 'The School of Faith', we think about perseverance, what it takes to sustain a process which is like 'walking on water'; how we can continue living from faith, rather than fear. Fear is the enemy; it is our only enemy. The gospel of abundant life brought Jesus into conflict with those who abused their power over valuable resources, as well as those who did not know how to realize the power of the resources available to them. As we refresh the vision and repeat the strategy, we understand that this process, the 'way' of Jesus, has the power of the mustard seed.

Attentive readers will notice that I have not addressed all the relevant material in Mark's Gospel and that I have only hinted as to how these themes might relate to the Last Supper, the Passion, the institution of the Eucharist as an act of worship, and the foundation of the Church. There is also the matter of how we read the 'apocalyptic' elements in the gospel, and how the unresolved contradiction between God's abundance and the suffering of the world is addressed by the Atonement.

In other words, I recognize that the 'environment' envisaged by the book, though a form of wilderness, is relatively benign. What happens when the forces opposed to Jesus and the gospel intensify from general adversity to a specific and murderous hostility? Is it possible for us to sustain this way of praying, working and relating in the face of torment and death? And if so, what is the 'bread in our hands' in those circumstances, and what does it achieve?

I hope that it will be possible to return to these questions in due course.

Chapter 1
A Way to Feed the Multitude

The day was drawing to a close when the disciples came to Jesus and said: 'What on earth are we going to do? There are five thousand of them. They are all hungry, and it will be night soon. We can't stay out here in the open. There's no food, no shelter. Nothing.'

And Jesus said: 'You give them something to eat.'

At which point they got angry: 'Oh yes? With what, exactly? We're tired and hungry too, in case you haven't noticed. We're like that because we've been working hard, doing what you asked us to do. And we're poor because we've left our jobs and homes and families to do it. We've nothing left to give. Get it?'

And Jesus said, 'Yes, I get it. What do you want to do?'

This confused them, because they had been so full of their anger, pain and fear that they had not been able to think beyond their feelings. There was a collective intake of breath. Some looked at Peter, some looked at the ground or the sky, some shrugged.

In truth, they were none too pleased that Jesus had asked them. It meant that they had to take responsibility for the situation, think out a strategy and put it into action when all they really wanted was for him to take the whole thing out of their hands and do something – anything – to make it right. They rather resented him doing this, and they were also uneasy because his words suggested that he might not know where the resources were going to come from, either. But, of course, none of them wanted to admit this.

In the end, someone proposed that the crowd be sent away into the surrounding villages where they might find lodging and food. But someone else said: 'If we do that, you know what will happen. Some will get lost, some will get distracted, some will get left out. The wild ones will start stirring up trouble, the judgemental ones will decide we can't cope and the vulnerable ones will feel we don't care. We'll lose them and we'll lose the moment. It will never come again.'

A third person said what everyone was thinking: 'So we've got to keep them together. But we still don't have anything to give them. And we still don't have any money to provide for them.'

Jesus said, 'How much food do you have? Exactly?'

They told him. Five loaves and two fish. Jesus said, 'So what do you intend to do with them?'

Someone said, 'That's enough for one person. Two at a stretch. We'll just have to decide who those two should be.'

Jesus asked them, 'Is that your best strategy?'

'I don't know about best,' the disciple replied, 'It's the only one we've got.'

'All right then,' said Jesus, 'I'm going off to pray. Let me know when you've decided what to do.' And he walked away.

The 12 disciples looked at one another, then everyone started talking at once. One thing they all agreed on, and quickly: half the food had to go to Jesus. But the other half, how should that be distributed? They all had their own ideas about that. They argued about it for hours, while night came down and the crowd began to drift away – the wild ones fighting, the judgemental ones criticizing, the vulnerable ones hobbling.

They were still arguing about it in the early hours, when all the people had gone except for those who could not move because they were too burdened or sick or frightened or frail. The night grew darker and the wind grew colder, and still the disciples could not decide how best to allocate their one meal, while children cried with hunger and an old woman died, unnoticed, under her thin cloak.

When day broke and the disciples saw what had been going on around them, they were distraught. 'What should we have done?' they asked Jesus.

'Brought it all to me. Asked me what I would do with it,' he said.

'But how would that have made any difference?'

'Try it next time, and we'll see.'

So, the next time, they did. There they were on the mountainside, with a large crowd, many of them in great need, and everyone hungry. Jesus said, 'How much food have you got?'

They told him: 'No more than we had before,' then asked, 'What are you going to do?' Jesus said, 'Get everyone to sit down.'

They did as they were told. And when he had fed the crowd – all five thousand people – with the five loaves and the two fish – and everyone had eaten their fill – and the disciples had gathered up 12 baskets of broken pieces – which, as Judas pointed out, was enough to give all of them a good meal with plenty left over – they asked him, 'Rabbi, how did you do that?'

And Jesus said: 'You don't get it, even now, do you? Faith is not about what you have. It's about what you do with it.'

Being sent and setting out

Each Evangelist tells the story of the feeding of the five thousand in his own manner. In Mark (6.30–44), the story is told in the context of the 'Mission of the Twelve'. Jesus has appointed 12 of his disciples to be apostles (3.13–18). Encountering incredulity and unbelief in his home town of Nazareth, he embarks on a tour of the nearby villages, teaching. During this time, he calls the Twelve to him and begins to send them out in pairs (6.6b–13).

For both Jesus and the apostles, this is a defining moment. For Jesus, it is a mark of his respect for these men, and the measure of his faith in them, that he is willing to entrust them with this task. For the Twelve, it is a commission that is both daunting and exciting. They have accompanied Jesus, listening to his preaching, watching him and helping him as he ministers to the crowds, but now they are to share in his mission as independent agents, working on his behalf, but out of his sight.

There is an enormous difference between observing someone else demonstrating the power of the gospel and doing the same thing yourself. There is a vast gulf between 'He can do this' and 'I can do this'. Venturing out is scary as well as empowering. We learn a lot by listening to someone talking about their work, even more by watching how they do it: but we learn most of all by doing it ourselves.

As we set out, there is a doubt which follows us like our shadow: will it work? Will it work this time? Will it work every time? Will it work for me? We may assume that this doubt is due to our inexperience, lack of education, training or whatever. We may assume that we are the only ones who feel it, but, in fact, the doubt will always be there, lurking somewhere in the back of our minds, however experienced or expert we become. In a television tribute to the comedian Tommy Cooper, one of his colleagues described how, throughout his career, Cooper was always anxious before a live performance. He could make people laugh simply by breathing into the microphone while he was still off-stage. But every time he walked out into the spotlight, he was terrified, because there was the possibility that this time, he would dry, bomb, fail – that this time, it might not work.

This doubt is part of any creative process – not just at the beginning, but at every stage of it – so it is wise to name it at the outset and to understand that there is no way to avoid it. Denying and suppressing the doubt only makes it stronger. Like a ball on a length of elastic, the harder you throw it from you, the harder it bounces back. If we make a habit of venturing out, this fear will always be with us. It goes with the territory. We can learn to manage it, but we will never overcome it entirely. The only way to deal with such doubt is to face it, make allowances for it and go ahead anyway.

It is this element of uncertainty which makes being sent out – or setting out – such an adventure; which makes the transition from hearing the word to doing the word so nerve-racking, but also immeasurably enriching. Hearing the gospel and watching others apply the gospel is exciting enough, but it is no substitute for applying it ourselves and discovering that the gospel will work for us. Yes, it is demanding, but discovering that the gospel works – even when I preach it – is exhilarating, humbling, awesome.

Our anxiety stems from the fact that the outcome of our venture is not under our control. Its shape is uncertain. We are acting ahead of the evidence, or despite a considerable amount of negative evidence. So the outcome – and the value of the outcome – remain in doubt. We cannot be sure where this road will take us. We cannot guarantee that the consequences will be clear-cut, beneficial or beautiful; that they will win the approval of our peers, match our own high expectations, or look like success.

However thoroughly we have prepared for this moment, there is a real possibility that the venture will not work. However diligently we have prayed beforehand, we must still reckon with this possibility, with our fear of it, and with how we might feel. Indeed, I would argue that it is an essential part of our preparation in prayer that we face all this. Having taken it into account, however, we go ahead anyway, because this is what it means to act in faith.

We do not act in faith by controlling events so that success is guaranteed, nor by suppressing, denying or in any other way avoiding the possibility of failure. We act in faith by reckoning with the full reality of failure, but going ahead despite it. We do the right thing, the courageous thing, the creative thing, even though we know it might not work. This is what faith is: taking responsibility for ourselves whatever the situation; take creative action – when necessary – ahead of the evidence; even being willing to take positive action in a negative scenario; but doing so with a clear head and open eyes.

Only by being willing to act in faith can we make the transition from hearing the word to doing it. This is what 'doing the word' is all about. Acting in faith. Living by faith. Living from faith, not fear. It is by facing our fears and still doing the best and most loving thing that we discover what living with faith, hope and love really means, and how living like this is 'good news' not just for us but for others, too.

We discover that living like this is possible, but at the same time, we discover precisely why it is so hard, and knowing this makes it much easier to understand why we and others resist the way of faith. We cannot just tell people to 'have faith' and expect them to respond positively. The invitation to act in faith arouses all sorts of fears in us that we must learn to recognize and articulate. Fear makes us very uncomfortable, and some of us already live with very high levels of anxiety. This is not our fault. Fearful people are wounded people. We have learned to be afraid because of the way that life has treated us. So we have to learn that we can manage our anxiety in small amounts and at a pace we can control. We need strategies for doing this and a supportive environment in which to do it, for we will only spend time with our wounds if we can see how this exposure will facilitate our healing.

The good news is that faith is always possible; that faith gives us access to an abundant life shaped by love. Faith makes this abundance available always and everywhere and to everyone, regardless of their circumstances, and even in the midst of adversity, suffering, oppression and death.

Jesus proved this by living the way of faith to the uttermost, even though it took him to the cross. Though he died on the cross, faith did not. His disciples discovered that even in the place where their hope had died, it was possible to respond with faith as he had taught them. However we understand the resurrection, ascension and Pentecost, they were – and they remain – experiences grasped by faith. They make sense in the context of Jesus' 'way' of faith. So Jesus is good news too.

During his ministry in Galilee, Jesus demonstrates how faith enables an ordinary human being to become a source of abundant compassionate, life-giving, life-generating creativity. Having spent time teaching his disciples and involving them in his work, there comes a point when he sends 12 of them out to do it themselves. Only by doing so can he – and they – find out how much they have learned; whether they can live the way of faith to the uttermost; whether, by acting in faith, they can meet the needs of the crowd.

Question: In which areas of my life and work do I see myself as 'venturing out' at present? What do I hope will happen? What am I afraid might happen?

Reflection: Jeremiah 1.4–10. 'Do not be afraid . . . for I am with you to deliver you, says the LORD.'

Called, commanded, sent,
I stand upon the brink.
Your name, my venture.
This is what I am formed for.
This is what I yearn to do.
This is where it begins,
the journey in light and in shadow,
walking your way,
facing my fear.
Setting out,

I wonder.
How far will you take me?
And how much faith do I have
in myself,
my companions,
and in you,
now that I have set my feet
to the road?

Travelling light

Mark tells us how, in sending out his apostles, Jesus 'ordered them to take nothing for their journey except a staff; no bread, no bag, no money in their belts; but to wear sandals and not to put on two tunics' (6.8–9).

I learned the wisdom of 'travelling light' on a trip to Greece as a student in the 1970s. I packed my rucksack in a hurry at the last minute, without giving sufficient thought to the difference between what I wanted to take, and what I really needed. I ended up with a pack that was so heavy that I could not carry it more than a few yards. This did not matter while we were still in England, moving from car to train to plane: it mattered a great deal once we were in Greece, where I had to walk a couple of miles at a time and get myself on and off the local buses. As the trip went on, I revised my opinion of what was necessary to me, and dumped many items in wayside litter bins, but even then my pack was too heavy to be comfortable.

Remembering this incident, it is tempting to interpret Jesus' words as the advice of an experienced traveller: 'Take no more than you can carry.' In fact his instructions go far beyond this. He implies that the apostles are not to take food for the journey, or money or a change of clothing or even any basic equipment, such as a bag to carry things in. They are allowed sandals and a staff, but that is all.

This is a level of denial that most of us would consider irresponsible. We would not consider travelling without money, credit cards, mobile phone, protective clothing appropriate to the conditions, and a change of clothing if we expect to be away overnight. Depending on the kind of journey we are making and the terrain into which we are heading, we might also take identification, maps, medicines, food, water, a sleeping bag or a tent.

From this point of view, Jesus' command does not make a great deal of sense. It raises the stakes: the apostles are being sent out on mission – daunting enough – and they are also being told to go without provision. Why is Jesus making this venture harder than it needs to be? Is he encouraging them to act irresponsibly? Surely not. But if not, then what does he mean?

This is the point. Jesus wants us to ask questions. Whether he expects us to take him literally, or is exaggerating in order to shock us, the effect is the same. He wants us to examine our preconceptions and reflect on our assumptions, to reconsider our response. He is challenging the way we see and think about what we are doing, why we are doing it, and in particular, how we do it. His challenge implies that mission is not what we do, but how we go about it.

So what we carry with us matters, because it reflects the way we see the task and the resources we believe we will need to fulfil it. The things we carry with us reflect what we believe about ourselves and our task, and about the One who has sent us. It says a great deal about the extent to which we have prepared ourselves for the journey.

The more luggage we take with us, the more we have to pay attention to it. If we have lots of bags, we have to find ways of lugging them around. If your suitcase is misdirected at the airport and ends up on the other side of the world, or if you lose your passport, or if someone snatches your handbag, then your entire trip can be put in jeopardy; at the very least it becomes a much more difficult experience. However, if we travel without baggage, we have the opportunity to pay attention to other things.

Of course, this will not be the case if we regret the things we have left behind, if we fret constantly about what we do not have with us, and what, as a result, we might not be able to do. Such anxiety fills our minds, distorts our perceptions and assumptions, and makes it hard for us to use the opportunities of the road. So it is not enough to jettison our excess baggage: we must also leave behind our fear of needing it. This requires a mental process of reflection, acknowledgement and letting go. It requires us to become more honest and self-aware. Travelling light is an attitude, a way of thinking, a creative dynamic.

Travelling light is a venture of faith. To obey Jesus' instruction, the apostles set out without knowing how their basic needs will be met. They have to rely on the generosity of those who welcome them and who will offer hospitality as a way of responding to the good news. Even if they make use of existing contacts – friends, relatives or acquaintances – and even though they remain fairly close to home in a culture where hospitality is offered readily and valued highly, there is still a large element of uncertainty involved. And uncertainty breeds fear. Will they be given what they need, when they need it?

In order to go at all, they have to act as if the answer is 'yes'. They have to acknowledge the doubt, and perhaps give some thought to how they will respond if they do indeed find themselves without food or shelter. Having done this, they go ahead anyway. They act ahead of the evidence.

This is why travelling light is a state of mind, because we have to be willing to think and act like this, and we are not always able to do so. We may not know how to do so, because we simply cannot imagine how we can travel without the things we consider to be essential.

This shows us the place where the problem lies, the place where Jesus wants to work with us. It lies in the way we are imagining the journey; what the road will ask of us and whether we will be able to respond. And if not, what will happen then.

Jesus wants us to imagine what might happen, and then to question our assumptions so that our hidden trains of thought are revealed. He wants us to bring our assumptions out into the light, where we can reflect upon them and ask whether they are, in fact, true. He wants to challenge the judgements we are making, and then to imagine an alternative, to see ourselves thinking, feeling, speaking and acting in ways we might not yet believe to be possible.

Question: Do I find it easy to 'travel light'? What is the 'excess baggage' I am carrying with me? Why am I reluctant to leave it behind?

Reflection: Genesis 12.1–9. What did Abram take with him? What did he leave behind?

I do not want to leave so much behind:
the things I want, the things I need,
the things that keep me clean and comfortable,
learning, working, growing.

I do not want to leave so much behind.
Each item has its purpose,
and pausing
to reflect – question – imagine an alternative –
only adds to the struggle.
Why should I bother?

I do not want to leave so much behind.
These things are like an extra limb,
an extension of myself,
a self so painfully conceived,
a self so carefully constructed.

I do not want to leave myself behind.
How can I do that?
How would I cope?

It would leave me alone
with my fear.

I do not want to leave myself behind.
If I am to make this journey,
I need these additions to myself.
They are my shield and shining sword
in this scary engagement
with the unknown.

But is this the only answer:
to hold on to so much
because I am so afraid?
Or can I really do this as I am,
myself,
alone,
unarmed and powerless,
knowing only that as I venture
within your purpose,
with your wisdom,
I am never beyond your sight?

Is this your faith alternative:
The narrow gate I would discover
if I trusted more;
trusted myself and others? You?
Would the world look different if I
trusted the things within me;
the self that is hiding
from what I can't yet handle;
that is yearning to believe:
longing to be born?

Knowledge that equips us

Let us consider the obvious: why do we take things with us when we travel?

We take what we believe will help us get from A to B in safety and comfort. From experience, research or the recommendations of others, we take what we believe will be useful on the way, and/or when we reach our destination. What we pack is determined by what we expect to encounter. Our luggage is shaped by what we imagine the journey will be like.

In general, this is good practice. Wearing suitable clothing and using appropriate equipment can prevent accidents and injury, increase our endurance, even ensure our survival. The more unusual, demanding or hazardous our journey, the more important it is to travel 'responsibly', by which we mean anticipating likely difficulties and being prepared for them, either by taking the right things, or by knowing how our needs might be met by other means.

To some extent, 'things' can be replaced by knowledge, especially specialized knowledge of the environment, terrain and conditions, both its hazards and its opportunities. Knowing how to recognize, access and use resources along the way, we can be more confident, flexible, creative and resilient. Our specialized knowledge equips us with strategies we can use to find the resources we need. So, whatever happens, we are no longer powerless, at the mercy of our context.

The survival expert Ray Mears can travel light in wild places because years of learning and experiment have taught him how to live off the land. He can make a long journey across country alone, on foot and carrying only a few basic items, because he knows numerous methods of finding food, water and shelter in the natural environment. The information and experience he carries in his head equips him for the journey. To some extent it replaces the equipment that he would otherwise need to carry.

His 'specialized knowledge' arises from a particular way of seeing his environment. Instead of seeing wild places as alien and uncomfortable, he sees them as full of resources which he can convert into food, drinking water, fire, shelter and tools. Everything he needs is out there; it is already given. His 'specialized knowledge' is a body of skills, experience and strategies which allow him to recognize and use these materials to fit his needs, and the needs of anyone who is travelling with him.

Does this apply to mission, too? Is there a form of knowledge, experience or insight that equips us to travel light in body, heart, mind and spirit? That enables us so that we can carry out our mission whilst 'living off the land'? Does it empower us to live – even thrive – in environments that others find barren or threatening?

Jesus' instructions to his apostles assume this is so. He challenges their vision of the environment into which they are heading. Do they see it as a harsh landscape, alien and comfortless, or do they see it as a world full of resources that they can receive with gratitude and deploy with skill to further the purposes of God? Will they recognize the gifts of God as they are given? Will they know how to make best use of them?

He implies that everything they need is already out there. They do not need to take bread, because bread will be provided. They do not need money, because everything will be given. They do not need to keep moving from one house to another, because the first house that welcomes them will resource them for mission in that place.

Mission begins with the way we see the world around us and everything in it. Mission begins with a particular kind of vision that enables us to see the landscape around us as full of resources. This allows us to develop a specialized knowledge, a form of experience which equips us. We learn how to convert whatever we find into material God can use. We acquire strategies which allow us to do this and, as a consequence, we can act as if everything we need to realize the kingdom in this place is already given. We do not need to carry it with us, because it is already out there. We learn to trust that God, through our environment and the people we meet, will provide whatever we need. Faith and experience reinforce the vision: all around us, we see gifts, resources, blessings, potential.

Such a vision – and the strategies which go with it – form the 'specialized knowledge' which enable us to travel light. This is the wisdom God gives us. The mind of Christ. This is faith as a way of creative thinking that allows us to see alternatives, consider a wider range of options, choose the most life-giving possibility, tap potential. This is faith which enables us to see what others cannot see, and act as if that vision is true.

Question: Do I see my environment and the people within it as full of resources? If not, why not? Is the problem that the environment is empty and the people are lacking? Or is it that I cannot see what is there, or how to develop it?

Reflection: Exodus 3.1–6. Moses learns to see his surroundings with new eyes.

This is how it begins:
with a fresh perspective on the world,
a vision of my environment
as containing everything I need
to make real the kingdom;
and the willingness to see myself
as a person God can use.
This may not be how others see me,
or how I have learned to see myself,
but God's perspective
is the second opinion which gives me hope,
which shows me I have other options:
that I can choose faith,

venture out,
take a new road.

This is how it begins:
a new way of seeing,
a new set of assumptions,
a particular way of holding
what is given, what I possess,
and what I find along the way.

This is how it begins:
as I re-imagine the journey,
see the landscape with new eyes,
reassess my resources,
reckon and reflect.
Not like a banker calculating profit,
but like a shepherd cherishing souls.

The one thing

Jesus urges the Twelve to leave so much behind, and to set out with just a single set of clothes on their back and the sandals on their feet, and therefore we can overlook the fact that he does permit them to take one other thing with them. 'He ordered them to take nothing for their journey except a staff,' writes Mark (6.8).

Why a staff? For those who are walking for miles over unmade roads and rough, uneven terrain, a staff is a valuable aid. It acts like an additional backbone, helping travellers to keep their feet on difficult or uncertain ground, and supporting the weak, the weary or the wounded. It can be used as a probe to feel out a passage across boggy ground; and it extends the reach of an arm if there is need to pull a fellow traveller out of the mire. It can be used as a defensive weapon against animal or human predators; and in the heat of the day it can prop up a cloak to provide a little shade.

A staff is useful in many different ways. Although it is a simple tool, it has a multitude of applications. Like the fabled Swiss army penknife, it is many things in a single compact form. The assistance it gives the traveller is so basic and yet at the same time so vital – perhaps making the difference between life and death – that it can be regarded as the one essential piece of equipment which makes the journey possible.

The staff is, therefore, both practical and significant. It is the 'one essential' tool which adds to the strength of the person possessing it, a fact that is recognized in the Bible, where a rod or staff symbolizes the idea of a more-than-human authority or greater-than-human power.[1] For example, the staff of Moses represents the power of God which flows through him (e.g. Exodus 17.5–6); while the psalmist imagines the protective power of God as being like a 'rod' and a 'staff' giving him comfort (Psalm 23.4).

There are other contexts in which we might consider a single, simple tool to be the 'one essential' thing which makes a journey possible. Personally, I rarely leave the house without a pen and notebook in my handbag, so that I can make use of any spare moments when I am waiting for someone to arrive or something to happen. Over the years, I have filled dozens of notebooks with scribbled questions, ideas, headings, paragraphs and drawings made in such odd moments sitting in a café, in bus stations, or on a train; and when I have been caught without a notebook, I have used napkins, bus tickets, envelopes, leaflets, the endpapers of the book I am reading or scraps of newspaper instead. As a writer the opportunity to pay attention to what is happening within me and around me is what makes a journey worthwhile. Jotting things down helps me pay attention; it is the way I think, relate and respond to the world and everything in it.

The 'one essential thing' we choose for our journey says a great deal about us, about what is important to us, and about how we see – or imagine – the journey. Other journeys require different choices. If Ray Mears were asked to choose a single tool to take with him into the wild, he would probably choose a knife: to carve other tools, cut and shave kindling for a fire, gut a fish or butcher an animal. In the wilderness, a good knife can make all the difference between death and survival.

Several years ago, I was involved in an exchange programme with Methodist women from Kenya. One of the visitors, Asenath, stayed in my home for a week. After a couple of days, I noticed all the women in the party carried large squares of bright cotton material. Asenath showed me how these squares could be used in many different ways, according to need. The square could serve as a shawl or an apron or a blanket. It could be twisted into a headdress or knotted to form a bag to carry shopping, or slung around the body to hold a baby or infant. It was a single, simple, flexible, multi-purpose tool, the 'one essential thing' which made the 'journey' of daily life easier.

When we consider our own 'journey' of daily life, especially in those places and situations where we are 'venturing out', the 'one essential thing' which Jesus urges us to take with us is faith. Faith is our 'staff', that single, simple, flexible, multi-purpose tool which is both practical and significant, reminding us who we are and what kind of journey we are making. It assists us in all sorts of different ways, giving us an additional strength which comes in many forms: compassion and creativity, courage and commitment. If we have faith, we can travel light, because faith supplies everything else we need. We can leave everything else behind, because faith is the 'one thing' necessary, that will get us going and keep us going, enable us to do the job and to survive.

Why faith? Why not love? The reason is that we are thinking here of faith as a spiritual tool which equips us for creative living. Love is not a tool and should never be used as a means to an end. We do not love because love is useful to us, or because it produces the results we want, or achieves what we want to achieve. We love because we love. Love is an end in itself; it requires no justification. If we try to qualify it, or insist that it submit to reason, it ceases to be love. As soon as we use love to attain anything or make something happen, we have stopped loving or, perhaps more accurately, we have fallen short of that high love which God revealed to us in Jesus Christ.

Faith is different. Faith must be shaped and defined by love, but it is not identical with love. Faith is a personal dynamic, a process, a way of discerning, imagining, believing and responding in order to create something new, better, life-giving; something that is rich and full, fruitful and free. Faith is the spiritual tool we use to generate abundant life. For ourselves and for others.

Question: Do I have one simple, flexible, multi-purpose tool that makes my daily life easier? Can I imagine how faith might be such a tool to assist me in practical and spiritual matters?

Reflection: 2 Kings 5.1–14. Naaman encounters a new way of seeing the world, and a different way of doing things, which allows him to be healed.

> To become wise,
> we clean a window,
> choose one thing to look at,
> and examine what we see.
>
> To understand God,
> question everything;
> then refine the question.
>
> If Christ's mission is a river
> flowing from the mountains to the sea,
> we do not ask
> how much water it contains,
> or how much farmland it irrigates,
> or how many people live
> on the food that land produces.
>
> No. Refine the question.
>
> How does the river flow?

What we see is what we get

I was brought up within the (Presbyterian) Church, and though I walked away from anything to do with religion for several years during my teens, I decided to become a Christian again at the age of 18, and I have remained within the (Methodist) Church ever since. I have listened to thousands of Christians talking about what faith means to them, and discovered that we see 'faith' in many different ways. Just as light can be refracted into a spectrum of colours, so 'faith' is not a single idea but a rainbow.

For some, it springs from inquiry into ideas of God, Jesus and salvation; for others, a personal relationship with Jesus Christ as our Lord and Saviour. Some emphasize an inner experience of power, the infilling of the Holy Spirit; while others define it primarily in terms of a rich, living tradition, or a loving attitude towards other people, or a reverent administration of the sacraments, or a commitment to justice and peace, or a way of cherishing the world and everything in it.

There are many ways of 'imagining' or defining faith, and it matters how we do it, because in the spiritual life what we see is what we get. The lens we use to focus on faith shapes our priorities, attitudes and beliefs. These tend to determine how we express our faith in words and action, and in turn, shape the way we expect other people – and the world around us – to respond.

For example, if we see faith as a set of ideas about God, Jesus and salvation, then our aim in mission will be to expound those doctrines, showing how they arise out of the biblical text and how they make sense of life as ordinary people experience it. We will focus on preaching, teaching, expository Bible study and apologetics. We will create an environment for discussion, argue our case and look for conviction.

If we see faith as a personal relationship with Jesus Christ as our Lord and Saviour, our preaching will present his life, death and resurrection in these terms. We will recount the evidence from the gospels and show how Jesus addresses the needs of people like ourselves. We will focus on developing personal prayer and fellowship groups so that people can grow in Christ. We will tell the story and look for commitment.

If we see faith as the presence of the Holy Spirit in an individual, group or context, then our preaching will exhort our listeners to be open to this experience, and to appreciate what it means. We will promote charismatic worship and prayer groups in which people can discover and use the gifts of the Spirit. We will guide and encourage them in so doing; and we will look for change.

Again, if we see faith as a loving attitude towards other people, as the administration of the sacraments, as a commitment to justice and peace or as a way of cherishing the world and everything in it, then we will preach and act accordingly. What we see becomes what we think and what we do, and this has a profound effect on the way that others respond to us, the manner in which situations unfold around us and the opportunities which open up for us.

These different ways of seeing faith are rooted in the subtle complexity of the human personality and the huge diversity of human experience. They arise from different combinations of the various parts of ourselves: our body, senses, emotions, memory, reason, imagination, purpose and spirit. We can use any of these combinations to focus on faith, but if we make our focus too narrow the vision it gives us will be very restricted. Indeed, if we develop our faith without reference to every aspect of ourselves and our experience, the result is a distorted form of religion: something that is all head and no heart, say, or something that is all transitory experience and mindless fluff. This is how the pure gold of the gospel becomes a debased currency – unhealthy and ultimately exclusive, both in terms of what we proclaim and what we practise.

Everyone I have met is in search of a faith that is sufficiently practical, adaptable, effective and inspirational to support them and nourish them in dealing with their problems. Many are convinced that they have found it, yet often, this conviction only lasts for a time. Most of us discover eventually that if our faith is to sustain us throughout a lifetime of learning and growing, worry and work, then our vision of faith itself must develop, change and deepen. We realize that our focus on faith has been too narrow, that we have been viewing faith through a lens of one particular colour, and that we must expand our vision if our faith is to remain sufficient for the challenges of the road.

For a faith that can sustain us throughout our lives and which will enable us to work creatively with others in addressing the problems of our age, we need faith like the staff of a long-distance pilgrim; that will assist us in a great many ways and give us access to a treasury of resources.

For this purpose, we need not just one or two of the colours of the faith spectrum but the whole rainbow. Each shade connects us with the Source of life in a different way; each offers us its own form of strength, challenge, inspiration and renewal. So faith is not only a creed to which we give intellectual assent, it is *also* a relationship with the living God in Jesus, *and* an experience of creative energy. It connects us with a contemporary community *and* earths us in a tradition; it inspires us in the celebration of the sacraments, *and* fosters our concern for the wider world in which we live, not least our care of the earth. Faith relates to every aspect of ourselves and the whole of our experience.

We need the whole rainbow because every aspect of ourselves is important. When I set out on a journey, I do not leave bits of myself behind, I take my whole self with me. We are called by God, and grow in faith, as whole people; we venture out in faith as whole people, too, although not one of us is whole in every sense of the word. On the contrary, we remain a mass of bruises and contradictions; flawed, fallible and frail. The vital fact is that we are oriented towards wholeness: we are walking towards it, however slowly, however much we falter, however often we take two steps forward and one step back.

This being so, only a holistic view of faith will enrich every aspect of our experience, allow us to develop life-giving relationships with a wide variety of people, and equip us to make a creative response to all of life's demands.

A holistic view of faith allows God the freedom to care for us as whole people. We are complex creatures: physical, emotional, rational, imaginative, purposeful beings, embedded in networks of relationships which require constant attention. If we see every aspect of ourselves as strengthening our faith, we allow God to love us whole. We allow every aspect of ourselves to be cherished by the Creator, saved by the Son and energized by the Holy Spirit. We become fully engaged, and as we persevere, especially as we allow ourselves and our faith to be formed by love, each part of us begins to interact more smoothly with every other part, so that as whole people, we become more fully aligned God-ward.

The process is the same as we form groups and organizations that venture out together. Imagining faith in holistic terms enables various selves to communicate and converge, to respect each other's integrity as well as each other's difference. God loves us all in our entirety, calls us together to become more whole, and leads us out on mission so that the diversity of creation can become a vibrant, vital unity of fruitfulness and fulfilment. We will resonate as a single chord, creating harmony, beauty, song.

Question: Which aspects of my personality are emphasized by my definition of faith? Are some aspects of my personality 'played down' or even ignored? Am I willing to explore them and let them grow?

Reflection: Jeremiah 18.1–11. Faith means allowing ourselves to be shaped by the potter's hand.

Faith is:
body,
emotion,
memory,
reason,
imagination,
will
and spirit.

Faith is:
the whole of myself
wholly directed
toward God.

Faith is:
relaxing,
healing,
renewing,
invigorating.

Faith is:
God's life in me,
a sure sign
of the Spirit's
presence.

Faith is:
me
becoming
myself,
filling my skin,
inhabiting my space,
telling my own story,
being filled
with the Spirit.

Faith is:
discovering
I am centred, poised,
ready, free
to give
myself
away.

Making a life of faith

When I was 18, working in central London, and about to go to Durham University, I started going out with a young man who not only attended church regularly but took his Christian faith very seriously: so much so that he had left his job in retail to work for a charity, taking a considerable cut in salary. The idea that someone could allow faith to influence their choices to that extent was a novelty to me. I had heard of such things happening in theory, but had never before met someone in my own age group who had taken that sort of risk: moreover, who was making a habit of it; making a life of faith from many acts of faith, large and small.

I was particularly impressed that he did it without bragging or making me feel uncomfortable because I made my decisions differently. We spent a lot of time sitting in a pub near Charing Cross, talking about the meaning of life. I found his attitude refreshing, intriguing and challenging, although I did get a bit irritated when we were out for the evening together and he insisted on talking to the homeless men we met on Waterloo Bridge.

The relationship did not last, but he taught me one vital truth: that to be a Christian is an act of faith from beginning to end. So it was that after a particularly difficult day at work I stared off into the darkness and prayed, 'God, I don't know whether you are there or not, but I'm going to live as if you are. With that decision, my Christian pilgrimage as an adult began. It remains an act of faith to this day.

The only way we can live a life of faith is by making such a life, day by day, hour by hour, moment by moment, as we take one step of faith after another. This is not so much a matter of what we do, but how we do it. It is not about what we have to live on or work with, but rather what we do with it, or, more precisely, how we go about what we do with it.

If life is a journey, then faith is whatever it is that gets us up in the morning, that makes us tolerably civil to the people we live with. It is whatever it is that gets us to work and makes us reasonably good at our job. It is the way we choose to spend our lunch-hours, how often we phone our parents and whether or not we flirt with the guy who comes to fix the photocopier.

If life is a river, how does the water flow? What gets us moving, keeps us on the move? What options do we think we have and how do we choose between them? What does faith allow us to be? What does it enable us to do?

All kinds of faith are capable of feeding and nourishing us so that we grow, mature and flourish, but some ways of imagining faith make it easier for us to be creative, to see what no one else is willing to see, make an unpopular decision, grasp a slender opportunity, stay on the narrow road, persevere with radical change. Some ways of thinking about faith foster a wider range of possibilities in difficult circumstances, give us a greater degree of flexibility when we address problems, maximize the resources we have to hand, and magnify the potential of our actions even as we take them.

This is what Jesus discovered: a way of seeing and thinking with faith, acting in faith and keeping faith which works with our natural human creativity, maximizing, multiplying and ultimately magnifying all possibilities. His genius was to understand that faith is a way of creative thinking; a process which engages all our powers, senses and emotions, and channels them in a way that increases the potential of our resources and our situation. This process can be applied in any given moment, regardless of the circumstances. In fact, it is a process which becomes even more effective – though at the same time more costly and challenging – as a situation deteriorates. In short, faith is the one essential thing which makes everything else possible, and even in the most testing circumstances it gives us access to the power of God, whose resources are vast beyond our imagining.

This is what the disciples learned from Jesus. From listening to his teaching, observing him and working with him, they learned how to see a situation, how to think about it, and how to act within it so that they were able to make the most creative response to any person, any context, any difficulty. This is what being a disciple of Jesus means: moving from being 'hearers' of the word to 'doers' of it; knowing how to apply his way of faith to any situation, with creative, compassionate and sometimes amazing results.

By means of this 'way' Jesus showed his followers how God would meet the needs of others, and their own needs, too. Then, from amongst his disciples, Jesus chose apostles, men who were so immersed in his Spirit, so moulded by his 'way', that they could represent him, make disciples of others, further his mission. He sends them out, telling them to take nothing with them but a staff, as if that is all the equipment they need. And he is right, because they are, in fact, fully equipped, with everything they need to fulfil the task he has given them. He has shown them how God will provide such basic practical resources as food, shelter and money. He has given them a form of specialized knowledge which replaces all the luggage they would otherwise need to take with them. It is this 'way' of faith which they will preach to those they meet, and demonstrate so effectively that their hearers will learn to exercise faith too.

Jesus' 'way' of seeing, thinking and acting with faith is the content of our training as disciples and the 'tool of our trade' as we venture out on mission. It is the means by which we make the journey, do the job, provide for ourselves and stay on the road. Whatever we need, the 'way' can provide, and if the problems we encounter prove to be greater than we anticipated, then the 'way' will show us where God is providing those extra resources as well.

Only Jesus' 'way' of faith will enable us to make a life of faith out of many acts of faith, so that the many aspects of ourselves, working together for a higher purpose, reflect the life of Christ. Like the Twelve, we set out empty-handed, carrying nothing but this 'way; but it is all we need: our message, our mission, and the means to achieve it.

Question: Who showed me what faith can be? How did they show me?

Reflection: Isaiah 50.4–5. God teaches us to listen and learn, and to speak, so that we may sustain the weary with a word.

It is not what we have,
but *what we do with it*,
that enables us to think
and speak and act like Christ.
How we walk the road,
receive its delight, face its danger.
All we take with us is the Way,
but the Way is all we need.
All we need to say,
all we need to demonstrate,
all we need to meet our needs
for bread and courage
and hope.
Forever.

Chapter 2
The Prospect of a Feast

During the festival, the town centre became a market, with stalls along every street, marquees filling the squares, and booths in every open space. Traders spread out their wares on pavements and steps, while hawkers wove through the crowd, selling goods from barrows and trays.

Every day, thousands of people came in from the surrounding countryside, thronging the approaches, converging on the market-place and the church behind it. There were signposts, but no one heeded them: they only had to follow their eyes and nose and ears into the heart of the town, where the crowd became a crush as people idled past the stalls, lingered and looked, bantered and bartered, while stall-holders pitched, pattered and bawled to attract their share of attention.

The market overwhelmed the senses. There were drapes of red, orange, yellow, green, blue, indigo and violet, while amongst them sparkled mirrors, crystal and glass. The metalworkers had pewter and tin, bronze and copper, silver and gold; the jewellers, diamonds, rubies, sapphires, emeralds, topaz, onyx and pearls. There were stalls that glowed with polished wood; others that were redolent with musk, perfumes and scented oils; and others where birds chirruped, clocks ticked and music played.

Every corner had its busker. Every other cabin had its craftsman – or woman – shaping or stitching while the passers-by watched, commented and questioned: shoemakers and candlemakers; carpenters and upholsterers; milliners and haberdashers. There were sculptors chiselling quartz, hacking at granite, forging steel. There were modellers working papers and plastics. There were pavement artists sketching portraits in charcoal and chalk, and dealers in fine art, offering luminous acrylics and age-darkened oils. There were calligraphers, printers, bookbinders and publishers. On one hand, philosophers debated; on the other, players raised a laugh; on all sides, the crowd was enticed by colour and clamour.

The town had always attracted adventurers who believed its streets were paved with gold. Now, for a few days at least, it was almost true. It seemed that everything was for sale, and anything was available to anyone – for a price. Here, those seeking their fortune could find the treasure that delighted them. If they could pay for it.

The thickest crowds were around those stalls selling food. First the butchers, in their vast blue aprons, chopping joints on worn blocks behind trays of cutlets, sausages and steak. Then the fishmongers, laying out the catch on beds of crushed ice trimmed with fresh parsley. And after them the greengrocers, fielding a harvest of fruit and vegetables on green baize. Then the bakers, filling their baskets with breads and pastries, puddings and pies.

And these were just the necessities. Beyond them, in the very shadow of the church, there was the finest part of the market: for many, the goal of their journey and the place where they glimpsed their heart's desire. Here were stalls of special luxury foods – tiny packets of self-indulgence, small parcels of exotic intensity – rich with heady smells. Sweets and spices. Caramels and creams. Fondants and fancies. Dark, aromatic swirls of chocolate. Fruits steeped in sugar and liqueurs. Here were hours of temptation, moments of bliss: the taste of heaven, wrapped in gold foil.

Everyone came to look, even those who could never hope to afford them. For here was a wealth they could understand: humble, life-sized, shaped to their basic needs and their ordinary longings. They could see its purpose, appreciate its power, enjoy its appeal. And it was only just beyond their reach. It was almost within their grasp. All they needed was more money. I wish. If only. One day. Dream on.

In the meantime, they could look. This was what had drawn them to the town, to the festival, to the market, to these stalls. This was what they had come to do. To look. To revel in looking. To gorge themselves with looking. To feed their eyes with the prospect of a feast.

No one knew where the traveller came from. No one saw him arrive. Only gradually did they become aware of him, standing on the church steps, launching his voice into the hubbub: 'Have you got what you came for?' he asked them, 'Do you even know why you are here?'

Ah, that was the question. 'Listen,' he told them, as people paused, swapping cynical grins and raised eyebrows, 'If you are thirsty, I know where you can drink. If you are hungry, I know where you can eat. As much as you want. Without having to pay. Good food, rich food. More satisfying than anything you can find here. Food that will fill you up. And you can get it for free. There will be nothing to pay! Isn't that good news?'

'Why do you buy these things?' he continued, gesturing towards the stalls where some of the trades people were beginning to look ugly. 'Do you even know why you want them? Because you have needs that are not met, and longings that are not fulfilled. You sense it, and so you search amongst the riches in this market to satisfy you. But do they do that? Do they fill you up? Are they enough? Do they even show you your heart's desire? In a way, perhaps. For a moment, maybe. But do they offer *everything* you need? Do they satisfy you in *every* way? *Forever*? I don't think so. So why spend your time and money here, when in a moment the enjoyment is gone, and you are hungry and thirsty once more? Why spend all you have on things that cannot deliver what matters most? Love. Peace. Security. Hope. Joy. Don't you want these things? Don't you work hard so that you can have them? So why have you so little to show for all your efforts? Why have you nothing in your life that will *last*? Nothing that will help you dream your dream?

'Hear me, and I will tell you all you need to know,' the traveller added. 'Learn from me, and I will show you where to find all you are missing. Come with me, and you will be satisfied. Follow me and you will be fulfilled – forever.'

What happened next is disputed.

Some say that nothing happened because no one took any notice. No one listened, so no one heard.

Some say that the crowd laughed, and a couple of louts pelted him with refuse, and the police warned him, that for his own safety, he had best get out of town.

Some say that there was a riot, with the crowd grabbing food off the stalls, tables being overturned, and people and goods getting trampled in the scrum. The traveller was arrested and fined for inciting the trouble, and on his release some men cornered him in an alley for a full and frank exchange of views.

What is certain is that the moment passed. The traveller moved on. And he was never seen in that town again.

The good news kingdom

Mark tells the story of the feeding of the five thousand in the context of the mission of the 12 apostles, which was itself part of Jesus' mission as a travelling teacher. For Mark, Jesus is a teacher who heals, rather than a healer who teaches. It is his teaching which prompts people to follow him: his ability to heal and exorcise is seen as demonstrating his authority to teach and the value of what he is saying.

At Capernaum, the weight and substance of his teaching astonishes his hearers from the outset. He carries the congregation with him, and they are convinced. When he silences and expels the unclean spirit that rages against him, it merely proves the divine origin and nature of his words: 'They were all amazed, and they kept on asking one another, "What is this? A new teaching – with authority! He commands even the unclean spirits, and they obey him" ' (1.27).

On another occasion, his hearers question his authority to declare that a man's sins have been forgiven. Of course, the point cannot be tested: what evidence can anyone produce to show whether this is true or not? So Jesus settles the issue by doing the harder thing. He heals the man's paralysis too. He demonstrates his authority in a manner that is plain to see (2.1–12).

According to Mark, Jesus teaches everywhere he goes: in the synagogue on the Sabbath, in private houses and in his own home at Capernaum, where we find him 'speaking the word' to a house so full of people that there is no longer room for them all, even around the door. He also teaches in the open, especially by the lake, where he borrows a boat so that he can address the crowd without being mobbed (3.7–10). This is the task to which he feels called. 'Let us go on to the neighbouring towns, so that I may proclaim the message there also,' he says, when Simon finds him praying alone in the dark 'for that is what I came out to do' (1.38). It is in the context of this itinerant teaching ministry that he calls his disciples, appoints some as apostles, and sends them out in pairs to proclaim his new, authoritative teaching.

But what was it? What did Jesus teach, why was it so effective, and why was its impact regarded as resonant with divine power?

Setting off for a long day's work, I notice that the post has come. I do not have time to open the letter before I leave, but I recognize the handwriting and know that someone I have longed to hear from has written to me at last. Her letters are always enjoyable, but I have been waiting for this one with particular eagerness because she has promised me some good news. Now it has come! That knowledge sustains me as I walk down to the station through the rain. At first the train is so crowded that I cannot get a seat, but the thought of the letter keeps me cheerful. Eventually, the carriage clears a little and I find a seat. Settling down, I open the letter and read it with mounting excitement. The news is even better than I anticipated. It fills me with gladness, like a bubble of pleasure which I carry through the day. It continues to rain, and my work is hard and difficult, but colleagues comment on my cheerfulness, because whenever I remember that news, it makes me smile.

The gospel was fresh and authoritative, in the first instance, because it was good news. In the first 15 verses of his book, Mark tells us that Jesus himself was good news (1.1); that he proclaimed the good news of God (or of the kingdom) (1.14); and that he urged people to believe in the good news (1.15). We recognize good news because it encourages, heartens and uplifts us. We warm to it, because it motivates us and gives us endurance. It prompts us to celebrate. If we are offering the gospel, it should have the same effect. It should encourage, hearten and motivate people in what we offer them, and in the way that we offer it. It should cause them to celebrate.

Of course, the process of giving and receiving is complex. People do not always want to receive, even when it is in their best interests to do so. They do not always know what they want, and even when they find it, they do not always claim it. They may have no idea what is good for them, or they may be surrounded by so many good things that they are unable to choose between the good, the better and the best. They may murder the messenger simply because, however genuinely good the news that s/he brings, they do not want it enough to overcome their fear of change.

Consequently, we can never afford to be complacent, or judgemental. If someone rejects our good news, why have they done so? Is it because they are actively choosing evil, or because they do not recognize the news as good? If not, why not? Is it because our presentation is unattractive, or that we are not offering what people need? Do people not know what they need, or have they been taught that they cannot or should not expect anyone to attend to their needs; or, worse, that anyone who promises to do so is out to con them?

Somehow, Jesus convinced people that his offer was genuine; that he could and would attend to their concerns; that he offered them help, not harm. He met them at the point of their deepest hunger. The things he offered changed their lives for the better; his teaching transformed their situation, whatever their circumstances.

Secondly, in terms of content, Mark tells us that the good news concerned God and God's kingdom (1.14): that is, who God is, what God is like, what God wants to do, and how God is going about it.

The 'kingdom' is a way of imagining the direction of events; of asking the question 'What is the world coming to?' and of pondering whether there is any purpose in the large narrative of our times. We may prefer another image, but the essential question remains. It is aroused by suffering, bewilderment and powerlessness; by discovering that the fault-line between quarrelling civilizations runs past our door; by the struggle to manage long term, large-scale, far-reaching change. It makes us tense and anxious, because however clever or rich or powerful we might be there are always forces which are stronger than we are; which can overturn our good fortune in a moment, and overwhelm us utterly. Whoever we are and however we protect ourselves, we cannot avoid, ignore or deny the terrible possibility of disaster. Not entirely. So is God with us or against us? Is catastrophe a punishment for our sins? Are atrocities a judgement upon us? In short, is an 'act of God' something to be welcomed, or feared?

Jesus offers an assurance which, we can speculate, emerges from profound reflection, some study of the Scriptures, his self-understanding and his experience, not least the awesome insight he received at the time of his baptism. The import of his message is this: that however baffling or awesome it might appear from our perspective, God's purpose is good news for the ordinary person. The direction of history is to be welcomed, not dreaded, because God is a loving shepherd to the flock, compassionate, generous and just; because God wants to meet us at the point of our deepest and greatest need; and because God is working within and through events to transform our situation. God will give us life, so we can look for the kingdom with hope rather than fear.

So from the outset we have the general thrust and tone of Jesus' teaching. It strengthens people and builds them up. It reassures us that – regardless of plentiful evidence to the contrary – the overarching forces which govern our lives are benign, merciful and compassionate; that it is worth getting up in the morning, raising children, investing in the future, planning ahead. He depicts God's governance of the universe in a manner which looks and sounds and feels like good news to the struggling, vulnerable soul.

In answer to the question 'What is the world coming to?' Jesus' answer is good news. God is loving; God loves you; God sees your need and wants to meet it in full. Even better is the news that this kingdom is at hand: not a promise for the future, but a reality which is accessible, available and achievable – here and now.

For Jesus, the time of waiting was over: filled up, fulfilled, complete. The suffering, bewilderment and powerlessness which accompanies such waiting could be minimized, sometimes even overcome. The time of God's action had arrived: the time in which fulfilment was possible; a plenitude that human beings could not discover by themselves, but which God would create in partnership with them.

Question: Where and when have I received good news? What did it feel like? How did I react?

Reflection: Isaiah 40.1–11. Good news for those who need reassurance, strength, light, direction, hope.

The kingdom comes from the future
into the here and now:
Godrealm,
a dazzling delight,
a bounty of blessings,
a generous glory.

The kingdom becomes the future
as we claim it here and now:
Godrealm,

not yet seen in its fullness,
but glimpsed
in the word or deed which assumes
it has already arrived.

The kingdom becomes
the wishes we weave
into the warp and weft
of who we are, where we are,
what we are doing:
a benevolent whisper
amidst the clamour
of the world's pain.

The kingdom becomes the future
by the way we claim it,
as we take up the task
of telling the story,
and acting as if it is true:
as we make it just a little more real,
here, where there are listeners,
alert, attentive,
ears tuned to the wind.[1]

Seeing the good news

During my third year in junior school, my teacher, Mr Weatherly, showed me the power of stories. He loved to read to the class, got us to explore poems by illustrating them, set us to writing a story each week, read the best compositions aloud to encourage their authors, and gave over the last session on a Friday afternoon entirely to any of us who wanted to entertain the class with a sketch or an improvised play.

I had always loved 'composition', from the very first time I had been set one, in primary school, not long after learning my letters. But now, as I heard my stories read aloud, and as I gauged my classmates' reaction to my plays, I learned that writing could be done well, that it could entertain people and influence them, that it could be a vocation. Mr Weatherly taught me the power of stories by getting me writing them, telling them and acting them out. By the end of that year, I had learned that this was something I could do, that I wanted to write to the best of my ability, and that telling stories would be the real business of my life.

How did Jesus convince people that he was sensible and sincere, that his message was genuine, that in him God would meet their needs? He showed them. He showed them what the 'good news kingdom' looked like and how that vision was made real. He showed them how the abundance of heaven is brought to earth; how the promises of God become a vibrant reality for ordinary human beings. He showed them so that they could see for themselves how much God wants to give, and how it is given. He gave them a vision and taught them to develop it. He gave them a strategy and taught them to deploy it. He told stories which brought the vision to life and involved those around him in acting as if its 'alternative reality' was true.

Where did it all come from? Mark tells us that Jesus came from Nazareth and was baptized by John in the Jordan, so it is reasonable to assume that Jesus learned from John the secret of finding grace in the wilderness. This revelation was then confirmed and brought to life by the experience of baptism. The vision which overwhelmed Jesus as he came up out of the water symbolized all he had learned: the eternally abundant love of God descending in a specific, tangible form – the form of a dove – and lighting upon him. And the voice made it all personal: God acknowledged *him*, approved *him*, empowered *him*.[2]

But would it work for him? This was why the Spirit drove him into the wilderness, where he spent some time – described in the traditional manner as a period of 40 days – applying and refining and reflecting upon all he had received. In the wild, his survival depended on his ability to practise what he had learned. As he faced the spiritual and physical dangers of the wilderness and overcame them, he discovered that the gospel was true: the desert could be a place of abundant grace, where the people of God are fed by angels.

This was the experience which formed him, but what is interesting is that he did not impose it on those who followed him. He taught, but he did not baptize; he showed them the kingdom, but he did not expect people to have dramatic spiritual experiences; he took his disciples away from the crowds to deserted places, but there is no suggestion that they were away for prolonged periods of time, or that they were exposed to wild beasts.

Instead, Jesus used simpler, more ordinary means to give people a vision of what the good news looked like and how it might become real for them. The distinction is of crucial significance. Jesus' teaching was not a secret knowledge, reserved for initiates or even for particularly favoured followers. It was a graded body of specialized knowledge about how the creative Spirit of God is at work: where and how and why.

One of the key factors that contributed to his popularity was that his teaching was accessible to ordinary people: young and old; sick and healthy;

rich and poor; men and women. In its basic form, it could be understood and applied by anyone. His disciples did not have to be young, educated, studious or wealthy. They did not have to belong to the leisured classes or a school of scribes or a priestly family. They did not even have to be particularly religious or holy. Anyone could grasp the essentials, practise them and develop them in their normal context. They did not have to leave home, detach themselves from their kin, deprive themselves of food or sleep or sex. Jesus' teaching was aimed at ordinary people leading ordinary lives, rather than at spiritual athletes. His methods were consistent with his message: that the riches of the creative Spirit are available to all.

In Mark's Gospel, Jesus does not use stories to illustrate his message: they are the message itself. 'With many such parables he spoke the word to them, as they were able to hear it; he did not speak to them except in parables, but he explained everything in private to his disciples' (4.33–34).

Jesus worked on the principle that if we want people to strike out in a new direction, we show them where we are heading and how we are going to get there. If we want someone to see what we mean, we show them a thing and invite them to examine it and explore it. If we want to teach them a skill, we demonstrate it and encourage them to try it, coaching them as they learn through their own experiments. If we want to foster an attitude, we model it, inviting their observations, discussing their feedback, and giving them opportunities to practise the role themselves. If we want them to be filled with a different spirit, we tell a story which encapsulates that spirit and act as if it is real, getting everyone involved and giving each person their own role to play.

A story has a structure, but what matters is what this structure contains. What is the story about? Where does it begin? What happens? Who is affected? Why? What are the consequences? The structure is only the framework or container for something that is alive, dynamic, on the move. It is this dynamic – expressed as the line of a plot or the arc of a character's development – which gives the story substance. It is the skill of the author or storyteller in expressing this dynamic which brings the story alive. They show us that something is on the move. They show us what it is, where it has come from, where it is going, and why.

A story is constructed in order to tell us what has shifted; how it has altered, whether it is still moving, and whether this is good or bad. The story shows us how particular characters react to these developments, and invites us to judge the quality of their response. As they respond, so they alter, and we – observing them, empathizing with them, identifying with them – move with them. As we move, so we are changed. This is the power of a story: it can move us at many different levels at the same time: emotionally, intellectually, imaginatively. And it can move us on.

All stories are about change: anticipated or threatened; change to be managed or overcome; to work through to and resolve, and which may have to be handled in a particular way if it is to be resolved well. The element which turns a mix of characters, events, dialogue and environment into a story is *movement*. Something is glimpsed, pursued, discovered. Something falters, fails, alters, becomes renewed. Something fractures and re-forms.

At some level, all stories are concerned with change and how we manage it. We tell stories about our experience to explain what has happened to us, to share the experience with others, and to involve them in our discoveries or in our distress. In a spiritual or religious context, stories are about transformation.

There is no doubt that Jesus' vision was appealing and attractive. Consistent with the promises of God, it fed people, encouraged and strengthened them; gave them hope, for themselves and their children, for their nation, for their time. Jesus portrayed this vision using stories and metaphors, so that his hearers could imagine it – see that it was good, a blessing they wanted to enjoy – and rejoice that it was at hand.

Jesus' stories did more than describe the kingdom, however: they allowed people to imagine and think about change, and to begin acting as if this 'altered reality' was real. His approach encouraged them to see that the mundane events and ordinary decisions of everyday life might be the basis for the same kind of story, explaining what has happened, sharing the experience, and involving others with us in it.

This was the purpose of Jesus' teaching: to change people's minds, the way they see, imagine, think, believe and behave. And this is why we retell his stories: to get people to imagine the kingdom, to think kingdom thoughts, and act as if the kingdom is here and now; changing their minds so that their lives can be transformed.

Question: What did I do today? Where? When? With whom? Why? How did I change, and why?

Reflection: Psalm 16. You show me the path of life.

God says, take my hand:
I will lead you to peace.
I will lead you beside still waters.
I will lead you to pasture.
I will lead you.

God says, walk with me:
I will show you my peace.
I will show you where love dwells.

I will show you my dream for you.
I will show you.

God says, trust my way:
I will fill you with peace.
I will fill your heart with my joy.
I will fill your soul with my treasure.
I will fill you.

God says, choose your path:
I will hold you in peace.
I will hold you when the storm blows.
I will hold you when the flood rises.
I will hold you when you walk through fire.
I will hold you in darkness and light.
I will hold you.

The feast of the kingdom

It was the fiftieth birthday party of a friend. There was a table laden with food – far more than we could eat – even though there were dozens of us there. There were drinks 'on the house.' There was another table piled high with gifts. There was a disco which filled the room with sound and stabs of hot, bright colour. They played all the old songs, the ones I loved when I was 17. I danced more than I have danced in years – exuberantly, joyously, recklessly. Others joined me and we formed circles, twirling, laughing and waving to each other. It was fun. I loved it. I ached the next morning, of course. But I loved it.

We celebrate by sharing abundance: by providing it and then inviting lots of people to enjoy it with us. We use abundance as a way of marking those times which are important to us – endings and beginnings and points of transition. We give abundance to say 'I love you', 'I honour you', 'I'm thinking of you' and 'I'm sorry'. We take abundance to the sick in the form of flowers or fruit. Feeling gloomy is an excuse for a treat. We withhold abundance as a way of punishing people, including ourselves. While we no longer bury our dead with their most precious belongings, we still feel it's important to give a loved one a generous send-off. It is not just the ceremony that makes a good funeral, but also the wake.

The images used on secular Christmas cards suggest that for those who do not recognize its religious character, Christmas has become a celebration of abundance itself. Trees dripping with tinsel; blazing log fires; heaps of presents; mantlepieces dressed with candles and stockings; drapes, streamers, swags of holly – all these are only the backdrop for the golden turkey, the dark plum pudding and the bottle of red wine. And while we may regret the expense, resent the stress, and feel more than a tinge of guilt at our self-indulgence, few of us opt out of excess altogether. The fact is that the love of abundance runs deep. Human beings are party animals. We relish a feast.

If there is one image which Jesus used more than any other to help his hearers see how God's kingdom could be good news for them, it is that of the feast to which all are invited. In Mark, imagery of bread, food, eating and feasting provides a visual spine for the whole Gospel.

The people of God are on their way to the promised land, the land of plenty, the 'land flowing with milk and honey' (Exodus 3.8). But in the meantime, they must travel through the wilderness, and here they meet John, who knows how to clothe and feed himself with the free bounty of the wild (Mark 1.6). John has discovered that despite its hardships, the wilderness is not a place of deprivation and hunger, but a place where God gives abundance.

Mark's account of Jesus' own sojourn in the wild includes temptation and peril, but says nothing of fasting. Instead, angels wait upon him, as they waited on Elijah (1 Kings 19.4–9). The Gospel is shaped around a series of meals and references to feasting. These include the dinner at Levi's house (2.15–17); the feedings of the five thousand (6.30–44) and the four thousand (8.1–10); the meal at Bethany (14.3–9) and the Last Supper, the Passover meal (14.12–25), which also looks forward to the experience of feasting in the kingdom of God (14.25).

Who has access to the feast, to share in the abundance that God provides? Jesus defends his disciples in their desire to feast rather than fast (2.18–20). If they are hungry, they should be allowed to eat (2.23–28). No one can claim that they are unworthy to do so, because God's plenty is accessible to all, including tax-collectors and sinners (2.15–17). Even the Gentiles share in the bounty, because there is more than enough to go around (7.24–30). Jesus is always pushing back the boundaries. His attitude can be summarized by glossing an old Methodist dictum known as the 'four alls': all need to share in the feast; all can share in the feast; all can know that they are welcome at the feast; and all should be allowed to enjoy the feast to the full.

As a result, he becomes angry when he sees his opponents using Scripture and tradition to deny God's children the bread that will satisfy them (Isaiah 55.2). He believes that what God provides, God wants people to enjoy to the full, and this belief shapes his attitude to the Sabbath, too. Jesus draws on the idea that the Sabbath is the crown and completion of God's creative activity, a weekly foretaste of the ultimate feast, a celebration which includes everyone in the community, even the animals in their stalls (Genesis 2.1–3; Exodus 20.8–11; Deuteronomy 5.12–15). The Sabbath is intended to be a benefit to humankind (Mark 2.27). It is a blessing, a space in which we are free to live life to the full.

The imagery of feasting is attractive because it is a form of abundance which appeals to one of our most basic needs. We all get hungry, so a feast is the most marvellous meal we can imagine: sufficient in quantity, quality and diversity to please us and everyone else. But a feast is more than just food. There are many other elements which turn a meal into a feast: dressing up, a special venue, the guests, decorating the room and the tables, giving and receiving gifts, sharing tales, telling jokes, playing games, music, singing and dancing. It is a time when people meet, form new connections and develop existing relationships. Feasts are occasions when we pay attention to one another and honour one another.

A feast is a holistic experience, feeding us in many ways and on many levels – all at once. This is vital – that is, life-giving – because we all need nourishment, not only to sustain our physical selves, but also to feed our senses, emotions, memories, intellect, imagination, sense of purpose and spirit. And in each case, a feast can offer us more than a sufficiency: it fills us up; it provides an abundance. We have more than enough to eat, and more than enough to feed us in every other way, too.

At a feast we are satisfied, replete; because what we have been given is 'enough', or more than 'enough', for every kind of need. As Charles Wesley put it: 'Enough for all, enough for each; Enough for evermore.'[3] Describing and envisaging a feast are ways of imagining large, even unlimited, resources, and the power which can command them. Simply imagining such abundance feeds us and strengthens us. We are encouraged as we fill our mind's eye with such a vision, even more so if we can catch a glimpse of it with our eyes at the same time; if in some small way we can touch it, smell it, taste it.

Seeing the feast answers the most persistent, worrying question of our existence: Will there be enough? If we can see the feast – even if we are only able to imagine it – we are encouraged, empowered and emboldened by the sight. It reminds us that God's power and resources are infinite and eternal. God is abundance; in other words, God has more than enough of any resource we might need to transform our situation and our circumstances.

Question: What feasts have I attended? What did I most enjoy about them? Why?

Reflection: Isaiah 55.1–3a. The promise: bread that satisfies me.

> What we long for is a feast:
> immense and various and prolonged,
> enough to feed
> every part of ourselves;
> enough to feed
> all that we are,
> all at once and always.

> What we long to do is immerse ourselves
> in abundance:
> plunge in as whole beings,
> heart and body,
> love and loyalty,
> spirit-mind.
> We long to be
> filled;
> we long to be
> satisfied;
> we long to be
> fulfilled.

> And our deepest hunger
> is for a food
> that will fit our need for purpose,
> direction, meaning;
> bread that will not only satisfy us
> now and then,
> but become in us a source of Life,
> feeding always,
> strengthening us whenever
> we draw upon it.

> What we long for
> is the Feast of Life:
> Life that gives life,
> and enables us
> to give life in our turn;
> Life that gives life
> in abundance,
> for all people.
> Forever.

The promise of life

After many hours' healing and exorcising, and perhaps a few hours' sleep, Jesus slips out of the house to pray. In a deserted place, in the long, chill, silent moments before dawn, he returns to the Source of the life which feeds him, encourages and empowers him. Perhaps he is still praying when Simon and the others find him. 'Everyone is searching for you,' they say. Perhaps Jesus would have preferred not to be interrupted, especially as their message expresses the anxious need of the crowd and, probably, also their own. Even so, he responds to their hunger with confidence and to their urgency with a plan: 'Let us go on to the neighbouring towns, so that I may proclaim the message there also; for that is what I came out to do' (1.38).

In his prayer, Jesus has met with God, the Source of life; God who affirmed him in his baptism and fed him in the wilderness. Now, like John before him, he must emerge from the deserted place to teach the people how to find grace in the wildest places, and lead them towards the promised land of plenty and peace. He is the connection between the life of God and those who seek it. He must prepare the way and make the path straight for them, so that they can find the life they need (1.2–3). The more that the depth and scale of human need is made plain to him, the further he will travel, the more he will enlarge his mission.

Jesus knew how the feast of God could be made available to feed the greatest human hunger; how the ocean of God's love could renew the well of a human heart; how the eternal light of God could pierce the shadows of the world. He knew the vastness of the resources at God's command, and the depths of the human condition, and he knew how they are connected. He showed that the connection is life: God's ability to give life, and the human longing for *more* life: appropriate to the person, their circumstances and the need.

'More life' means different things to different people. For Simon, Andrew, James and John it meant a vocation rather than a livelihood. For one man in the synagogue at Capernaum, it meant freedom from the spirit within him which raged against Jesus and his teaching. For Simon's mother-in-law, it meant rapid recovery from a fever, allowing her to celebrate the remainder of the Sabbath with her household. For a man with leprosy, it was the fact that Jesus touched him, restored him to the human community, made him clean.

To some it means a new life, or a new beginning. To others, it means a better life, or a greater quality of life. It can mean the gift of life for someone about whom we are concerned; the ability to be creative, or the ability to endure. To anyone, it means satisfaction, fruitfulness, fulfilment, contentment, peace.

There are qualities which make us feel more alive, that give us our personal vitality and determine our quality of life. They shape our energy into the particular form most appropriate to the task in hand: love, understanding, strength, joy, ideas, peace, discernment, wisdom, patience, flexibility, kindness, generosity, forgiveness, grace, hope, faithfulness, justice, gentleness, courage or self-control.

These qualities are not 'optional extras'. They are 'food for the journey'; they make it possible for us to travel in faith, hope and love. They are the elements we need if we are to weather our difficulties and resolve our problems in a creative manner; if we are to develop healthy relationships, connect with those around us, build a just society, care for the earth. They are the resources which enable us to live fully, freely and well, regardless of our circumstances. As such, they not only benefit us, but empower us to become a blessing for others.

The trouble is that we do not always possess them, or possess them automatically. Some we acquire through nature and nurture, but none of us has enough. As we bear with our own moods, as we interact with other people, and as we engage with the wider world, we are drained and exhausted. We are worn down by weariness, work, uncertainty, anxiety, illness and sorrow. We are knocked about by other people's indifference, torn by conflicting loyalties and confused by complexity and change. We are battered by anger and hatred, guilt and loss.

Even when we feel 'full of life', we may know we will need it all – and more – to face the next challenge. The more we are conscious of wanting to live life to the full, and of wanting the same for other people, the more we become uncomfortably aware that in many situations, life is in short supply. All those resources which give life can seem so limited in us, in our communities, in the world.

As we grow older, we may feel that life is a finite resource, and we tend to fear this limitation. And the more we fear it, the more we feel bound, imprisoned, depleted, drained. Gradually, we understand that we are caught in a continual conflict between energy, creativity, liveliness and generosity on the one hand, and disease, deterioration, destruction and death on the other.

The struggle between life and death permeates our whole existence, and at every moment, we monitor where we are in the struggle. As we face problems, adversity, challenge or change, this question becomes more urgent. Do we have enough of those resources which will give us the particular kind of energy we need to do what needs to be done?

The greater the threat, the more this becomes the only real question. Do we have enough life in us to get where we want to go, to empower us to go ahead? The greater the difficulty, the more urgently we ask ourselves if we have the resources which will equip us to cope: resources that will give us 'more life'; if possible, a glimpse of abundant life.

Question: What forms of 'hunger' matter most to me? What forms of 'more life' do I need to satisfy me? Can I see where God is supplying an abundance to encourage me?

Reflection: 1 Kings 4.7, 20–34. The scale and variety of riches available to the king.

> The feast of the kingdom
> shows us the scale of God's store,
> the scope of God's largesse,
> the magnificence at God's command:
> a wealth of food,
> a profusion of life-giving things.
> The provision fills our eyes,
> fills our mind, long
> after we have ceased to look.
> Years later, yearning,
> we retain it.
> We can remind ourselves.
> Remember.
>
> And remembering, we feast again
> as those who were among the first to arrive,
> as those who have never left,
> as those who are seated at the highest table;
> as those whose bellies are always empty
> and whose hands are always open,
> ready, waiting to receive.
>
> Remembering, we have life.
> The life we need.
> The life we want.
> The life we asked for.
> The infinite promise of more.

Longing for life

As a writer, I am never happier than when I am facing a blank page. As an artist, I get a delicious tingle of anticipation whenever I set up a fresh canvas. To be provided with empty space and permission to fill it with all that pours out of myself: that is a wonderful thing to me. During decades of creative activity, I have rarely had any problems coming up with ideas. Completing them and getting them out into the world has been trickier, but that is another story.

When I was 10 years old, I had chickenpox over Christmas. My mother remembers that I was quite ill, but what I remember is waking up on Christmas morning to find a new exercise book in my stocking. In those days, a red Silvine exercise book cost me a whole week's pocket money, so it was a valuable gift to me. And I appreciated it for another reason, too, for by now I was in Mr Weatherly's class, where I was learning the power of stories, writing and words.

As I looked at that first blank page, I decided that I would not waste this notebook by simply scribbling in it. I would use it for a Special Purpose. I would write a Book. The Book would be a story (of course). It would be my first Book, the first of many. I would write it for myself, but one day my Book would be Published, and then I would become a Writer.

Looking back, I see how we create all kinds of problems for ourselves when we dignify our dreams with capital letters, but even so, I cannot ignore the importance of that moment. It was the birth of my dream; my vision of what feeds me, fills me and fulfils me; my personal image of abundant life. My dream may not matter to anyone else, but it matters more than almost anything else to me; because it gives me life. It has formed me and continues to inspire me and motivate me. However well someone knows me, if they do not know this about me, then they do not understand me, who I am, what makes me 'tick'.

All of us need 'more life'. Whoever we are, we need to find our way to the Source of life. Though another person can point the way, in the end we each need to know for ourselves how we make that journey. Our dreams, desires and longings are vital because they help us 'imagine abundance' for ourselves, and in the process, they point to those particular elements which give life to us. Out of all the many good things I could do, and the many beneficial ways in which I could spend my time, it is writing which connects me with the Source of life and which enables me to express that life, not only for my own sake, but as my way of enriching our shared experience of the world.

However, for many years, although I longed to devote more time, space and energy to it, I could not believe that my writing had spiritual significance. I assumed that it was just a human or worldly ambition, and like many serious Christians, I had a problem with that idea. In fact, I felt slightly guilty doing anything simply because it fed or enriched me. It was years before I allowed myself to believe that these occupations showed me how I, personally, made the journey to the Source of life, and that God wanted me to make this journey again and again.

Why? Because whatever gives us life is necessary to us, and God wants us to have those resources which give us life. We need food of many kinds to feed and strengthen us. Having a dream or a longing or a large desire builds your sense of yourself, who you are and what you can do. Food of this kind establishes, develops and sustains your confidence, your sense that you can take action, accept the reactions of others, amend your behaviour as necessary, do this better next time. It enables you to understand that you can do this, and do it well, as your contribution to the project, the group, the goal.

When we know which elements, situations, activities and dreams connect us to the Source of life, we know how to find our way to that 'more life' we long to receive. Even if you are not – at present – able to 'live your dream', it is vital that you know what your dream would be, because the particular elements which give you life can occur in many forms. They can be shaped to fit a wide variety of circumstances and can be pursued in many different ways, one of which will fit your circumstances at this time. Your 'large desire' can point you towards a wide range of activities and interests amongst which you will find companions for your journey, mentors to inspire you and resources to replenish you on the road. In the end, you will discover that your situation, as it is now, already contains materials you can use to help you 'imagine abundance' for yourself. And all the elements which give us life are connected. As we grow rich in one, we grow rich in them all.

The amount of time we devote to pursuing our dream can be less important than the fact that we know what it is and pursue it at every opportunity. Our dream, our treasure and our large desire is an expression of our human longing for life, a life lived to the full, infinite and eternal. It is a way of 'imagining abundance' for ourselves, in a way which makes sense to us. This is not necessarily selfish: it can enable us to make our contribution to the ongoing life of our family, network, congregation and society as a whole. By feeding us, it gives us resources with which to feed others, and to ensure that the world is fed.

Question: When and where do I feel that I am in touch with the Source of life? What is my 'dream'? Do I feel free to 'imagine abundance' for myself? If I do not yet have such a vision, am I willing to invest time in developing one?

Reflection: Psalm 36.5–9. The love of God: a fountain of life and light.

This is what the love of God is like:
faithfulness that is true, steadfast and sure,
as high as the heavens;
more vast than the countries in the clouds.
This is what the love of God can do:
discerning the depths of the abyss,
it draws all things into the right way,

saving them from death,
giving them the fullest life.
This is how the love of God feels to us:
as the care of one who knows us, welcomes us,
embraces us, shelters us – shelters everyone –
under a warm, protecting wing.
This is what the love of God offers us:
life that is full, like a feast in good company;
like wine from a sparkling river;
like water from an endless spring;
a fountain of life and light.

The way of faith

Jesus was 'good news' for ordinary people because he convinced them that God, the Source of life, longed to feed them with everything they needed for a full, rich, satisfying life; a life of freedom and fulfilment; that would be 'enough' in every way and forever. His teaching was authoritative because he not only gave them the prospect of a feast, but showed them how it could become real. He told stories which started them seeing, thinking and acting as if this 'alternative reality' was true. In helping them to 'imagine abundance', he fed them with life-giving resources.

The more we 'imagine abundance' for ourselves and for others, the more we receive the creative resources which strengthen us to act as if such an abundance is real; and which enables us to follow Jesus in making it personal, practical, material and specific.

The more we 'imagine abundance' for ourselves and for others, the more we are fed with those life-giving elements which enable us to respond to a situation and make the best of it; which help us to face the challenge, assess an obstacle and find our way around it. These elements give us the resilience to work through our problems rather than avoiding them and equip us to manage change so that it is creative for everyone involved.

The more we 'imagine abundance' for ourselves and for others, the more riches of various kinds we see: not because the world changes all at once, but because the way we view the world begins to change. Where once we saw our environment as barren and ourselves as impoverished and depleted, now we begin to feel resourced and resourceful. We may not yet see how we can use what we have, but at least we can see what is available. This way of seeing and thinking about the world is of crucial importance, because the more we see ourselves as resourced and resourceful, the more confident we will be, and the more we can act in faith.

Confidence comes from seeing ourselves as having the resources we need. These might be resources within us, such as energy, strength, ideas, creativity, flexibility, resilience, endurance and courage. They might be outside ourselves, such as money, people, tools, space and time, the recognition and support of our peers and our superiors, a favourable environment and so on. We might have access to both kinds.

Confidence comes from seeing ourselves as having enough: to manage what needs to be managed; to change what needs to be changed; and to achieve what needs to be achieved. At the very least, we need enough to do what needs to be done at once – to take the first step, or to complete the next – but we prefer to know that we have enough to complete the task to our satisfaction, or in a manner that will win the approval of others. If we are facing a really tough challenge, we prefer to know that we have plenty, more than we need: an abundance.

Many of us have a problem with the idea of 'confidence'. Sometimes this is because we lack confidence ourselves, and we are suspicious of what we do not possess. Sometimes, it is because we have been bullied by those whose 'confidence' was actually arrogance. Sometimes it is because we have known people whose 'confidence' is due to an extrovert personality, or has become a means of hiding a sump of pain.

However, truly confident people are not arrogant; in fact, they are the opposite. They do not need to boast, belittle others, insist on their own way, or throw their weight around to get their work done or make their mark on the world. They trust their character and achievements to speak for them. They know that they can meet their own needs and influence events without being unpleasant. They have a sense of their own value, and so they trust others to recognize their worth. They are not 'full of themselves' because they are full of other, lively and life-giving, things instead; and from their 'fullness' they give to others. They give freely and generously, and their giving creates gratitude, trust and friendship, rather than anxiety and obligation.

We can recognize a truly confident person because they are stable, secure and grounded. They are comfortable in their own skin. They are open to new ideas and willing to change, but they are not blown hither and thither by other people's expectations or opinions. They encourage others, and in a discussion will persuade them without resorting to fawning or flattery. They are good to have around because in any company and in any circumstances they are positive, hospitable and creative.

Confident people are resilient. They have an inner strength which allows them to face challenge and change, threat and adversity. When they are knocked back, they do not crash, they bounce. They can sustain their morale despite suffering and struggle. They feel pain and grief and anguish like anyone else, but they have a buoyancy which gives them the capacity to endure.

Confidence is the quality or state of having faith, of acting in good faith, of living by faith, of keeping faith. A confident person has faith in themselves, in others and in the larger powers that influence and govern our existence. Whether or not they believe in God, they have an essential confidence in life and in the way that life works out. They have faith in humanity, in the goodwill of others and in the ability of good people to overcome the hazards and problems we face in the world. They trust themselves to make good choices, and trust others to do the same.

Confident people inspire confidence in others because they see other people as abundant rather than inadequate. This enables them to build relationships based on trust. They will be assertive if someone tries to trample on them, but they also know that they do not need to be assertive all the time. They are happy to step back, to make room for someone else to take centre-stage, and coach them until they feel at home there. They are those of whom we say, 'They have restored my faith in human nature.' They help us to have faith in ourselves and in one another, because they show us how faith can help us make a creative response whatever our circumstances.

To apply faith to every aspect of our experience, all at once, all the time, can become complicated. But it is a skill worth learning, because faith enables us to marshal all our powers towards our goal. It is the gathering of our energies for a purpose, the harnessing and focusing of all our abilities to see, imagine, reason, remember, commit and create, and the directing of all those energies into worship and service.

What we experience is heart, conviction, potency, enthusiasm, excitement, possibility. What we communicate is life.

Question: Do I have the resources I need for what I face at the moment, or for what I need to do?

Reflection: Isaiah 40.27–31. A life that renews our strength.

A long way from the Promised Land,
from where I want to be.
The desert at my feet:
a road of change.
Afraid.

Not sure I know enough;
not sure I know the right things:
where the wells will be,
the food I need,
the shelter, friendship.
Always at call, whenever?
Always enough?

I am not alone.
Bearing others, I also bear
their needs besides my own.
Bearing the world,
I hunger for good news,
restless to live the Way
this one man lived.

Have I set out too soon,
before I have learned enough?
What it means to give?
How to get through?
No, the question is
how to do more than survive;
how to live fully, bravely, brightly;
how to find your milk and honey land.

My treasure. Your glory.

Chapter 3
Meeting the Multitude

Of the thousands drawn to the festival, hundreds visited the church beyond the market square. Most came to learn about the history of the building, marvel at the carved pillars and stained-glass windows, buy souvenirs in the gift shop and eat lunch in the café. Very few came to pray.

This angered those who ran the church, for they regarded themselves as the custodians of the greatest of all treasures, and they had spent their whole lives guarding, conserving, researching and explaining its power, while their congregation dwindled away. In general, they were good people, who longed for others to recognize the value of the treasure, acknowledge its significance, and give thanks to God as the Source and Giver of all good things. But they had lived in the church so long, immersing themselves in its images and ideas, its language and its ways, that they no longer understood the multitude.

The mystery that they regarded as a treasure, the crowd in the marketplace saw as remote and irrelevant. To them, the mystery was not only unfathomable but also alienating. It was an unreachable absolute that offered no practical improvement to their lives. It made demands on them that they felt they could not possibly meet. However pure their intentions, however hard they tried, it remained beyond their grasp. And when they failed to measure up, they felt condemned by a Judge against whom there was no appeal.

Some of the younger members of the team, being ardent, inexperienced and idealistic, wanted to change the treasure into a form the crowd could accept: something practical; something that would feed them, heal them, give them joy. They argued that God did not intend the treasure to be kept locked up in the church, however much it was revered there, but to be used to help others. They were prepared to give it away.

At this, some of the older members were furious, saying that the power and value of the treasure lay in the very fact that it had been fashioned in ancient times, that it had existed for millennia, that it had been passed down unaltered and that it had never changed. Others were more sympathetic, but shook their heads, saying that they had tried to reform the treasure many years ago. A part of it had been melted down, reminted and offered to the public at a great festival. In fact, this was the origin of the festival which still drew thousands to the town every year. But offering the treasure had not led to an increase in devotion. The crowd had simply consumed everything on offer and gone, leaving their litter in the empty streets.

Some, who had been ardent and idealistic in their day, had become embittered by a sense of profound failure. Most, however, were just discouraged and sad. They tolerated the festival, shook their heads over its excesses, put up posters to advertise their services, and rented out space on the steps to some of the more respectable merchants. Otherwise, they stayed in the church, leading services, welcoming visitors, managing the shop and the café, and only occasionally going to the doorway to see what was going on outside.

And so it was a while before they realized that a travelling prophet had set up his soapbox at the top of the church steps. Arriving late, when he was well into his proclamation, they did not hear all his message. In the confusion created by his speech, they lost sight of the man himself. And afterwards, when he had disappeared, and no one knew what had happened to him or where he had gone it was hard to sift fact from rumour.

Some said he had taken to the hills, to live amongst the vagrants who camped out in the wild. Others claimed he had moved to a neighbouring town, and was drawing large crowds to a rival festival. Still more asserted that he was a known criminal wanted by the police, and that a reward had been offered for information leading to his arrest. Yet another story alleged that the prophet had been beaten up in an alley, and that one of the men responsible had been a member of the church leadership team, a suspicion that made the team leader very angry, and which he denied.

The festival ended. The crowds went home. The town returned to its regular rhythm of life, and within a few months, the visit of the prophet had been forgotten, except in the church, where one of the younger members of the leadership team sought an interview with the leader to announce his resignation.

'But why?' asked the leader, aghast. 'You have a position here. A vocation. A career. Why throw it away?'

'I want to find the prophet.'

'The prophet? Whatever for?'

'I want to hear what he has to say. I want to know what he knows.'

'But he doesn't know anything! He has no education, no scholarship, no expertise. He is a wastrel, a vagrant, a traveller.'

'He knows what we do not know. He knows the crowd. He knows why they are drawn to the market. He knows why they are searching, and he knows what they want to find.'

'Everyone knows that! They're greedy and selfish. Enslaved by their appetites. Ruled by lust.'

'No. That's the mistake we have been making. That's why they do not come to us. Because we have never asked them what they want out of life. We assume we already know.'

'What they want is something for nothing!'

'Exactly. And we despise them for that. We say we know better. But we should be learning from them.'

'Learning from the mob?'

'Yes. They come here to find life. Health. Fulfilment. Prosperity. Something that satisfies them in every way. Abundance – that's what they're searching for. They're looking for abundant life in a form that makes sense to them.'

'They expect to find that in a market?' the leader spluttered in derision and disdain. 'You think that salvation can be bought in a shop? Have you learned nothing from your time here? From your studies? The liturgy? Our prayers?'

'No, I don't think that,' the young man explained patiently, 'and they know in their hearts that they will not find it there, as well. But they don't know where else to look. And they don't come to us, because what we offer them doesn't look like what they're searching for. It doesn't look like abundant life. It doesn't even sound like good news most of the time. How does it offer them life – let alone a life they can live to the full? We don't even know that ourselves. We've lost the art of it. We need to regain it before we can make our treasure accessible to the people.'

The team leader, who was now a regal shade of purple, burst out: 'Anything he knows, we know.'

'On the contrary, I don't think we even know how to ask the right questions,' replied the young man.

'Questions are easy. If you have them, ask them. We've been researching the answers for hundreds of years.'

'That's the problem. Here, we are still answering the questions as people were asking them hundreds of years ago. I want to answer the questions as people are asking them now.'

'But the questions never change.'

'No. But perhaps we have to find out where they are leading us today. Find out how to follow them. Make our own journey. Discover how to start from here.'

The leader shook his head in despair: 'You want to go out into the wild in search of a madman? An ignorant traveller? But why?'

'I want to learn how to follow the promise of abundant life.'

'But look what happened to him! Nobody listened. They're saying he got beaten up! Do you want that to happen to you? Do you honestly think its worth it? If he has all the answers, why isn't everyone following him?'

'I don't know, but I think he does. I think that's why he asked people to go with him – why he asked people to *follow* him. Because he knows we can't recognize the treasure straight away. We have to open our eyes – learn to see it – learn to follow it – learn how to make the journey.'

The leader shook his head again. 'But follow him? A traveller? For all you know he could be dead!'

'No, he's out there. Somewhere. Whatever happens, I will keep going. Because even if he is dead, the treasure is alive.'

The power to deliver

Like Jesus, the Twelve travelled around the villages, teaching. Mark tells us that they proclaimed repentance, cast out many demons, anointed with oil many who were sick, and healed them (6.12–13). This was Jesus' intention from the beginning. He had given them authority over unclean spirits (6.7). Indeed, when he appointed them as apostles, it was to 'be with him, and to be sent out to proclaim the message, and to have authority to cast out demons' (3.13–15).

So the mission of the Twelve was a success. The work of the apostles, like that of Jesus himself, was authoritative and convincing. They had a sound grasp of Jesus' teaching, and they were able to demonstrate its truth and power, liberating people from the forces which dominated them, even those which were generally beyond human control.

It is reasonable to suppose that they modelled their methods on his. So it seems a little odd that Mark, having established that Jesus proclaimed the good news of the kingdom and instructed people to believe in the good news, says only that the Twelve 'went out and proclaimed that all should repent'. And that in the few verses he takes to describe their commissioning, he mentions their engagement with demons or unclean spirits no less than three times.

Whether these emphases originated with Mark or with Jesus himself, we have to ask what it is that Mark wants us to see? Clearly, whatever else the apostles taught, and whatever else they did, their proclamation of repentance and their ability to cast out demons was significant at the time, and to Mark more than a generation later.

To begin with, what does Mark mean by 'repentance'? The Greek words usually translated as 'repent' or 'repentance' refer to a profound change of heart, direction, purpose and spirit; equivalent to gaining another mind. John the Baptist preached 'a baptism of repentance for the forgiveness of sins' (1.4–5). Confession and baptism expressed a readiness to receive this 'other mind'.

To our eyes John is an ascetic, but to Mark he was a man who had discovered how God gives food and clothing in the wilderness. He drew people to join him at the Jordan – a great river in a land which has few permanent streams – and invited them to immerse themselves in its life-giving waters, so that they could receive God's bounty. He represents the call to abundant life; the wisdom of the wilderness that even in the desert God can provide what we need to live. He shows people an alternative future, and encourages them to see themselves as having the opportunity and strength to take it.

In the short term, he was authoritative and convincing. Large numbers were baptized, and some remained his disciples. Jesus travelled from Nazareth in Galilee to hear him, and he too was baptized. Herod and Herodias were convinced enough to feel threatened and act against him. Mark even reports that Herod protected him in prison, 'knowing that he was a righteous and holy man. When he heard him, he was greatly perplexed; and yet he liked to listen to him' (6.20).

John could not deliver the blessing itself, however. He could show people the kingdom, but he did not have an adequate strategy for making it real. He addressed people's need for forgiveness, but not their other needs for bread or healing or peace. He offered them a way of expressing their longing for change and their commitment to it, but had no means of altering those habitual ways of seeing, thinking, feeling and behaving which caused them to sin in the first place. He could not tell them how to persist in their good intentions, nor help them when they faced challenge, adversity or fear. He did not – could not – set them free from forces that overpowered them.

Once someone had received John's baptism, where could they go? How could they continue to live in the 'new reality' he had shown them? How could they persevere in the new direction he had set? Some found a way forward in more rigorous discipline and more frequent fasting (2.18), and it is also possible that some, like Jesus, followed John's example and lived in the wilderness for a time, to discover how the desert could feed them. But these approaches would not appeal to the majority. Rigorous discipline and desert living are not forms of spirituality attractive to the masses, for whom life is usually hard enough already.

Jesus' teaching had greater authority because it embraced both vision and strategy: a vision of the abundant life which God wants for us all; and a strategy which made the vision real in personal, practical, tangible ways, and which could go on doing so. The vision was good news because it offered the general hope of a better future; but the strategy was good news because it gave each person a realistic possibility of receiving 'more life' in the way which mattered most. Bread for today and bread for tomorrow, too.

It was this combination of vision and strategy which gave people a reason to believe that Jesus' audacious claim – that the life of God could be made real, for anyone, whatever their circumstances – might be justified. It showed them how they could begin 'following' that promise: acting as if it were true. It showed them how the process worked; how the power of God could make a difference; and it showed them how they could apply it themselves.

This is why Mark emphasizes the Twelve's ability to cast out demons, because he wants us to see that they have absorbed not only Jesus' vision, but also his strategy. And they have learned how to apply it. The gospel worked for them. They were able to confront and overcome any force which might threaten, dominate and control a person: personal or political; social, psychological or spiritual. They could not only teach what Jesus taught: they could do what he did. They had the power to make the kingdom real – the power to deliver.

Question: Are there situations from which I long to be liberated, forces from which I yearn to be set free?

Reflection: Jeremiah 30.1–9. Rescue, restoration, redemption.

> I want a gospel that works for me:
> is that selfish?
> I know the gospel worked for Jesus,
> for the apostles,
> for Paul and Barnabas and Timothy and the rest;
> for the saints and martyrs and witnesses down the ages;
> for contemplatives in their cells
> and evangelists on the street.
> I know all that, and I am grateful,
> because all that they said and wrote and did
> inspires me, feeds me, keeps me in hope.
>
> But that was then, and this is now,
> and here in this place, in this moment,
> in these circumstances,
> there are so few of us;
> and so little of me.
> There are times when it is hard to believe
> that the Creator has called me,
> that Jesus is with me,

that the Spirit will lead me on:
because (to put it bluntly)
I am working long hours,
investing everything
and getting nowhere.

Which is why I say,
without wanting to be selfish
or obstinate or rebellious,
that what I want,
for myself and for those I serve,
is a Gospel that works.

A gospel that works when we preach it.
A gospel that works when we apply it here.
A gospel that works when we turn to face the world.

A gospel that works for me.

The hunger of the apostles

On their return to Jesus, 'The apostles gathered around Jesus, and told him all that they had done and taught' (6.30). They are dazzled by the amazing, exhilarating fact that through their action, the gospel has allowed the abundant love of God to touch this person in this situation at this moment with transforming power. John had promised that the one who came after him would baptize people in, or with, the Holy Spirit (1.8), and Jesus had promised to teach them how to work with people (1.17). Now they have seen the promised power at work. They have much to tell.

However, they also need to eat and sleep. They need to rest and relax for a while. But they cannot do this where Jesus is working: 'For many were coming and going, and they had no leisure even to eat' (6.31–32). Mark makes a similar comment at an earlier point in his narrative, when Jesus is also at home, surrounded by the crowd (3.19–20). On that occasion, there was so much hubbub that incoherent stories reached the ears of Jesus' family, who came from Nazareth, intent on restraining him. We can also glimpse the scene in another story, when, during one of Jesus' teaching sessions, four men arrive, carrying a friend, paralysed, on his bed. The house is so full – the crowd spilling out into the street and clustered thickly around the door – that they cannot even attract Jesus' attention, let alone reach him. So they climb up onto the roof and dig down through the mud-brick until they create a large hole, through which they lower the man (2.1–12).

It is likely that Mark intends us to remember these episodes: he wants us to imagine a small house filled with disciples and besieged by petitioners, with Jesus at the centre of it all, listening, speaking, teaching and healing. No doubt there was much good work being done, but in this context Jesus cannot prioritize the apostles' need for quiet, nor his own need to be with them at such a time. So he proposes an alternative. 'Come away to a deserted place all by yourselves and rest a while,' he says (6.31).

Notice that it is Jesus who proposes the idea, not the apostles. He sees their need to recentre themselves; hear again the call that underlies their vocation; unpack and understand what has happened. He knows that there are questions which cannot be addressed amidst noise and confusion; that however vital or necessary our work, we need pauses when we slacken the tension sufficiently to reflect on our experience, pay attention to our responses and invest in an appropriate amount of self-care; and that we cannot do any of this unless we are willing to prioritize our own needs when necessary.

By putting this need into words, Jesus makes it possible for the apostles to see it and feel it. It is a measure of his respect and care for them. He sees their hunger, even if they do not. He sets aside the expectations and demands of others – all those lives that he could possibly change – in order to invest time and energy in them, and to encourage them to invest in themselves. He honours them by taking seriously their first independent experience of mission, and by recognizing its effect on them. They are hungry; they need to eat and sleep. They need to be heard at depth so that they can examine and explore all that has happened and all that is at stake. They need to be fed in every sense of the word.

Jesus could have simply taken them to a place where they were not yet known, but instead he invites them to go with him to a deserted place. This is significant. It implies the desire to get away from the crowd and its demands. It is not the familiarity of home that is the problem, nor the noisy bustle of street and market-place, but the unrelenting pressure of other people's need.

This is where Mark begins his version of the feeding of the five thousand: with the apostles' need to be fed; with the hunger of those who are living by faith, who are serving God, preaching the word, caring for others, administering resources, envisioning the kingdom. It points us to the meaning and purpose of the story – and indeed of the Gospel Mark has written, namely: where do we find the food that enables us to continue in ministry?

This is not just about the physical demands of the apostolate, or rather, not only about our physical needs. This hunger is the need of the whole person, the depletion that leaves us physically and emotionally drained, mentally exhausted and spiritually shattered. It is the depletion of our creativity, imagination and empathy, which, if not countered, ends in our feeling that our wound is incurable and overwhelming; that we are burned out and have nothing more to give.

Of course, the apostles are not yet in this state. But Jesus wants to prepare them for the possibility that, one day, they might find themselves in such a condition. He wants them to understand that they do not need to fear the desert; any kind of desert. They need not avoid the desiccated landscapes of their failure, depletion or fear. On the contrary, as the people of God have discovered from the beginning, it is in the places of hunger that God meets us and feeds us with the bread that supplies our need.

Question: Can I build on existing 'pauses' in my day to address the questions which cannot be asked amidst noise and confusion? What are the factors which make it difficult to do this?

Reflection: Psalm 131. The pause of stillness, quiet and humble trust: of feeding and being fed, of being filled and fulfilled.

> Here it begins:
> with myself;
> as I am, today;
> where I am,
> this place,
> this moment.
>
> These hands,
> stretched out,
> are open. Empty.
> Waiting
> to be held, helped,
> comforted, consoled,
> guided, sated.
>
> Waiting.
> Here. Now.
> Always.
> Needing you.
> Waiting.

Grace in the wilderness

In his build-up to the feeding of the five thousand, Mark uses the phrase 'deserted place' not once, but three times (6.31, 32, 35), as if to emphasize that, while it might not be the deep desert, it is a desolate spot, away from habitation: the kind of place, in fact, where Jesus likes to pray (1.35). For Jesus, this is a return to the wilderness; for some of the apostles, perhaps, a first encounter with the wild.

An isolated, desolate location acts like a great mirror, reflecting back to us our hunger. If we cannot see how this environment can feed us, the landscape looks arid, empty and forsaken. We imagine ourselves starving to death, becoming weak, helpless, abandoned and alone. The more we stare into this emptiness, the more we become afraid.

We go into the 'deserted place' to recognize this fear and learn how to confront it, so that we no longer fear any kind of 'desert': not the loss of our possessions nor the restriction of our freedom; not the ending of a relationship nor a betrayal of trust; not the deterioration of our health nor the failure to achieve our ambitions; not the breach of our security nor the destruction of our community. We go into the 'deserted place' to discover how we apply Jesus' way of faith – both vision and strategy – to every context, and to discover how this process generates the most dramatic results when the situation is at its most difficult and our resources are at their lowest ebb. God meets us in the wilderness and feeds us with a bread that meets our need.

This is the 'wisdom from the wilderness' which Jesus probably learned from John, but which Jesus expanded and developed in his own teaching as a vision and a strategy for making the kingdom real, always and everywhere. It begins with the ancient, remembered truth at the heart of the Hebrew scriptures: that 'The people who survived the sword found grace in the wilderness' (Jeremiah 31.2). It challenges those prejudices which restrict our vision of a 'resourceful environment', asking us to look again at the place where we actually live so that we can see the plenty God has given there. It asks us to look again at those people, things or situations which we currently dismiss as 'inadequate' or 'not the right kind' or 'not enough to meet the need', and helps us to see how they might be 'enough' to begin, to take the first step, to invest in God's process of change. It asks us to trust God – and God's process – so that what we invest has space to multiply and so to create abundant life.

The value of small things, of few, of almost nothing, is a lesson that only the desolate places can teach us. We do not learn this wisdom so well in prosperous circumstances or in the time of our power, which is why it tends to arise from amongst the poor and the marginalized; from those who know themselves to be weak, ill, disadvantaged or oppressed; or from those who have had the courage to strip away the conditions and assumptions of affluence and learn how to live as the poor do. It is when we are 'hungry' – when we do not have 'enough' – that we learn how to look again at the resources we have; how to see and think about them, apply them and keep on re-investing them until they have grown to meet the need.

This wisdom teaches us, in essence, how to survive and flourish, how to find 'more life' in such unrewarding circumstances; how the very ways of seeing, thinking and acting so that we can thrive in the wilderness can be applied to generate abundant life for all.

Question: What is the 'shape' of my hunger? Where do I worry that I am not 'enough', or that I do not have 'enough' to meet the need?

Reflection: Jeremiah 31.1–6. God's everlasting love and enduring faithfulness.

Hungry,
because I have not yet learned
the lesson of the journey,
or I cannot yet see how to apply it
to this moment, these circumstances,
this need.
Here. Now.
Hungry,
because I have not yet learned
how to let the way feed me;
how to work in a way that fills me
with the life which will do
what needs to be done.
Hungry, because I need to rest.
Even though I am excited, awed
by all that has been achieved,
I am also overwhelmed:
more drained than sustained.
Hungry.

Room to breathe, regain
that necessary illusion of control.
Room to receive, learn
how the desert can feed me;
how to find food in the wilderness,
so that there is plenty
for me,
for us.
Room to discover that
even in barren places,
and in my times of desolation,
God is awesome,
God is amazing,
God is abundance,

God is all I need,
all we need
between us.

Bread for our hunger.
Bread to share.

Learning how we are fed

It is in the wild that God meets us. Like Abram, we venture out; or like Hagar, we are driven out; or like Jacob, we flee. We go on a journey, or we are taken away from our normal surroundings, or we are shocked out of our routine, or we make a bid for freedom, or we go into exile. We are alone, or we feel alone, isolated by our experience, responsibilities, intentions, fear. Literally or metaphorically, we find ourselves in an environment which is 'outside' the familiar, away from civilization, uninhabited, inhospitable or simply far from home.

We go into the 'deserted place' to learn how we are fed. We may assume that we know this already, but the very nature of the 'deserted place' requires us to interrogate the obvious. So we re-examine those assumptions which govern the way we see the world, the opportunities available to us, and the choices we make. How does God feed us? How do we ask for what we need? How do we receive it when it is given? How do we share it with others? How do we give it away?

To ask such questions is like entering our own private maze. The insights we uncover are complex and confusing. We can lose our sense of direction. We are tempted to turn back. We wonder if we are making any progress at all. We learn that any one of these simple behaviours is far more complicated than it appears to be.

We learn to ask by asking. As babies, we cry because we are hungry or cold or uncomfortable. We ask for food and for the other things we need to survive, but at the same time, we 'ask' for the reassurance that we will be protected and provided for. We ask: 'Will someone care for me?' If our cries meet with a positive response, this reassures us that we will receive what we need when we need it. This gives us the feeling of being loved; it reassures us that we are lovable.

Throughout our childhood we 'ask' and from the reactions we get, we draw conclusions as to whether we are likely to get a positive response. We learn to adjust our requests so that we get more of what we need, or at least a response of some kind. If our request is met with coldness, hesitation, mockery, criticism, abuse or violence, we may learn not to ask at all; or we may learn that we can only get what we need by deceit or manipulation, by allowing ourselves to be abused or by inflicting violence on others.

More usually, we learn that some sorts of 'food' will be given, but that others are not available because resources are limited. We are told that we cannot expect to receive everything we want, because there is not enough to go around. We are told that 'money doesn't grow on trees' and that 'the world doesn't owe you a living'. We are told not to be selfish, not to be ambitious, not to want things too much. We are warned not to dream, because dreams never come true.

Or we may be told that we can have what we want, but only if we are very good, if we work hard, if we do what we are told at once, do all our chores first, do the job perfectly, ensure that what we do is all our own work.

From such responses – especially the ones we receive most often – we draw conclusions about when and how we can expect our needs to be met, or not. At the same time, we get a sense of when and in which circumstances we are loved or lovable; if at all.

We internalize these ideas, so that they become part of us; assumptions that we never notice, let alone question. At the same time, and in a similar way, we absorb ideas about how we should receive what we are given; how – or whether – we should share resources with others, or give any of them away.

Assumptions like these determine the extent to which we feel 'resourced' and 'resourceful' and, consequently, determine our confidence, or lack of it. Many of us who are taught in childhood that we must never be 'demanding', find that as adults we are unable to 'ask' for what we need from our partner, from our peers, from those in authority or even from God, no matter how desperately we may need it. This has a profound effect on our ability to maintain loving relationships, sustain a healthy work-life balance, negotiate with colleagues and develop our most life-giving talents. It also skews our relationship with God because all our ideas about what it means to ask, to receive, to share and to give are distorted.

Our personal understanding of such basic ideas shapes the way we see ourselves, the situations in which we find ourselves, and the options available to us. Moment by moment, as we ask ourselves, 'Do I have what it takes to deal with this?' it is this set of internalized ideas which answers the question before we know we have even asked it – and which therefore determines our response.

It takes time and diligent attention to unravel the way we think about such things. It is like following a path through the maze of our own thoughts, habits and prejudices. Sometimes we discover that, underneath our assumptions, there are memories which must be healed or hurts which must be forgiven before we can move on. But this is vital work, the very stuff of learning how to ask of God, receive from God, share with God, give to God. As we learn to ask, so we learn to pray.

We can grow beyond our assumptions. We can transcend them. We can learn that the love of God is not limited. God will feed us with anything we need, and honours our dreams, our longings, our large desire. Held in God's keeping, we can ask and receive; we can know that we will always be resourced; we will always be loved; we are seen as lovely, beautiful, valuable, worth any investment. As beloved children, made in the image of the Creator, we can collaborate more precisely with the Spirit as she generates abundant life. We have a share in the abundance that is being created; there is enough for us and for everyone else too, for evermore.

Question: How have people responded when I have asked them for resources that matter to me? How have these responses influenced my freedom to ask for what I need?

Reflection: Jeremiah 31.7–14. God's people will be satisfied.

> We go aside,
> not to avoid the crowd,
> nor to deny its hunger,
> but to meet our common need
> by other means.
> We go aside: so that God can meet us
> where life is always found,
> at the margins, in the spaces
> where we do not think to look.
> We go aside: to ask for bread,
> and in the asking,
> glimpse the feast prepared for all.
> We go aside: to receive
> with hands and hearts held open;
> welcoming, sharing, giving
> as others
> become willing to ask,
> as, together, we learn what it means
> to ask, receive, share, give.
> We go aside: to gather
> fine things in clay jars;
> treasures of eternity;
> passed on to us
> with trembling hands.

Meeting the multitude

They have left the work behind so that they can get away from the demands of the crowd. They take the boat and sail to a deserted place, in search of solitude. Silence. Stillness. Space. The companionship of others who have 'been there'. The particular attention of Jesus himself. His acceptance and approval; his affirmation and encouragement. Another glimpse of his vision; a deeper insight into his teaching. They are hungry, needing food for body, heart, mind, will, spirit. Even if they did not see their need before, Jesus' putting it into words has helped them to recognize it, and the journey has given them time to feel it, and to realize that it will only deepen until it is satisfied.

And then they see the crowd. The multitude is there ahead of them. They too are hungry. In fact, they are starving, famished for a word, a touch, understanding, peace; for a hearing, healing and hope. The depth of their hunger has brought them out into this deserted place, and they have brought friends, relatives, colleagues, neighbours. There are thousands of them.

What happens next is crucial. The plan is wrecked. The opportunity for some rest and recreation has been postponed indefinitely; at worst, it has been lost altogether. How do they respond?

The apostles have changed. They are no longer – if indeed they ever were – passive recipients of Jesus' teaching. Now they share with him a specialized knowledge that the crowd does not possess: a deeper understanding of how the gospel works and an experience of putting it into practice, of using the 'way' of Jesus to generate life for those they meet.

Knowing all this, they have a greater sense of responsibility. Now that they know something can be done, their assumptions have changed. Now that they know how much more is possible, their expectations of Jesus and of themselves have increased. Now that they know how to apply the 'way', they see the crowd as expecting a response from Jesus; but also from them. Whereas once they would have identified with the crowd, now they have begun to identify with Jesus. The apostles feel that the crowd is wanting them to act, but the scale of the task has multiplied; the need is so much greater now, and they themselves are hungry. Spent. Consequently, they see the crowd in terms of their demand. Some part of their concern is for Jesus, because they now know the cost of ministry, but they are also feeling the crowd's demand upon them, as his disciples.

When they look at the crowd the apostles see the breadth and depth and height of human need, to which they feel they have to respond. As they make their subconscious assessment of the resources available to them, however, they do not see how they can make a creative response. As they see it, they do not have the energy, the capability or the strength within them, or amongst them.

When we are faced with a challenge which we see as being far beyond our capability, we become anxious, and then angry. We sense that, if we are forced to meet the demand, we will deplete ourselves to an extent which threatens our health, our sanity, our faith, even our very survival. So the challenge is not only overwhelming in itself, it is also a personal threat, because to respond we have to put ourselves at risk.

Our will to live is so strong that it overrides almost every other consideration. We can set it aside, but only for a short time, in exceptional circumstances, and only to ensure the safety of something, or someone, we treasure far more than life itself. We cannot, will not, sacrifice ourselves on a daily basis. And if we feel that this sacrifice is being asked of us too often or too lightly we become angry; we feel it as an injustice. That we are expected to sacrifice ourselves at all implies that we are expendable. That it is for no real purpose implies that we are worthless.

Wanting to live, we see the crowd through the lens of our hunger, with the result that our reactions are dominated by fear. The need of the crowd appears to be infinite; its demands unlimited and relentless. We do not have the resources to address suffering on such a scale. Whoever we are, whatever we have, whatever we know, can never be adequate.

The trouble is that, if we see people primarily in terms of their needs or their demands, we are just one short step from seeing them only in those terms: that is, as defining them as needy and demanding. When we define who they are, we also limit what they can become. Our vision of them and of their potential becomes embedded in our behaviour towards them. How we see them becomes how we relate to them, and the character and quality of our relationship determines what we can create between us.

The way we see other people shapes our relationship with them. The process is subtle and usually subconscious, but if it proceeds unchecked it has far-reaching consequences. For example: how did the disciples feel when they saw Jesus giving his attention to the crowd? It was he who had suggested the journey to the deserted place, implicitly promising them the attention they needed. Now it appears that he is putting the needs of others before the needs of his close associates. The disciples could have felt justifiably aggrieved and sorry for themselves that the crowd was coming between them and Jesus.

All this is speculation, of course, but such a dynamic would throw into sharp relief the attitude of Jesus, who, on going ashore and seeing the great crowd, 'had compassion for them, because they were like sheep without a shepherd; and he began to teach them many things' (6.34). It also suggests a context for what happened later, when the disciples approach Jesus, saying: 'This is a deserted place, and the hour is now very late, send them away so that they may go into the surrounding country and villages and buy something for themselves to eat' (6.35–6).

'Send *them* away.' The crowd has become 'them' not 'us'. The apostles now regard themselves as a separate group, set apart from the crowd, distinct from it: even, perhaps, in competition with them for Jesus' time and energy. If so, their concern, which appears reasonable enough, masks another agenda. They want to regain control of the situation, salvage something from the wreck of their day, get Jesus to themselves and remind him why they came out in the first place. They are jealous and possibly resentful. After all, they have just completed a successful mission on his behalf. Doesn't that entitle them to some of his time? Why hasn't Jesus kept his promise? How can he so easily set them and their needs to one side, when they have made so much effort to help him?

Perhaps this is why they intervene. The hour is late, the light is going; there is no more time. The disciples started out hungry; now the crowd is hungry too and no one has any food. It is a deserted place; everyone will have to walk some distance to a village where they might be able to buy supplies. There is no other way that the crowd can be fed. There is nothing more that can be done.

In other words, they see a limit and so they draw a line. In so doing, they themselves become a boundary, a barrier, a wall. They step between Jesus and the crowd. They act as if the limit is real, and their action makes it real. They see a dynamic which is running down, and act as if it is all over.

Yet, since the moment Jesus began teaching, a process has been at work amongst the crowd which has not yet run its course, and so has not yet yielded its full potential. Who knows what Jesus has started here? Who says that nothing more is possible?

The disciples are determining – limiting – the extent to which Jesus can work with the crowd, and also the extent to which the crowd can think and act creatively, whether as individuals, small groups or as a single unit. Because the disciples are unable to see themselves as life-givers in this situation, they are unable to see any life in the situation at all. Because they feel ill-equipped to bring life into this particular context, they are unable to see how anyone else can do it either. Because their vision is distorted by their hunger and their fear, they are unable to see how they – or anyone – can supply enough life to meet the apparently infinite need of the crowd. All that they have learned about the power of the gospel, by which they have been trained and commissioned, is overwhelmed by hunger – the crowd's and their own.

Jesus sees their lack of confidence and nails it: 'You give them something to eat,' he says.

Question: Is there a situation in which I feel overwhelmed; responsible for meeting a 'multitude' of needs? Am I really the only person putting 'life' into the situation? Am I limiting the potential of other contributions by the way I see them?

Reflection: Song of Solomon 2.8–17. Arise, my love, and come away . . .

Go aside:
imagine a feast for us;
a pool in the desert,
blue water, green grass,
palm trees spreading shade over us,
broad tents,
open to tempt a breeze.

Go aside:
imagine a feast for us;
bread to match our hunger,
water to quench our thirst,
oil to pour on wounded souls,
wine to let the spirit sing.

Go aside:
imagine a feast for us;
a table laden with good things.
Enable us to see it,
encourage us to work for it,
equip us to provide it,
empower us to share it.

Go aside:
imagine a feast for us;
an echo of Eden,
our little patch of paradise,
an acre of the City of God;
the garden where nations
speak peace to one another,
imagining a feast for the world.

Choosing abundant life for all

Jesus says: '*You* give them something to eat' (6.37).

The idea is unreasonable, unfair, even offensive. Where does Jesus expect his disciples to find enough food to feed all these people, let alone the money to pay for it? But the provocation is deliberate: he wants them to think about their assumptions. What are they asking? What are they doing? Where is this attitude taking them? What will it achieve? Is this what they want? Do they have other options?

His suggestion exposes their powerlessness and challenges them to confront it. This is a 'kairos' moment: a place of choice, decision and judgement, when the situation hangs in the balance. Moments of choice have the potential to create profound change. The path divides, perhaps in opposite directions. Depending on our next move, the action could go either way. So the next step is critical: which way will our choice take us? Towards life or towards death?

On what basis does Jesus make his choices? All we know about his motivation at this point is that he has compassion on the crowd because they are 'like sheep without a shepherd'. This does not necessarily mean that he considers them to be weak and woeful. Rather, it indicates that, in his view, they lack the kind of leadership they need. Indeed, it might suggest that he sees the crowd as pregnant with potential, needing only a particular kind of leadership to flourish and be fruitful. So Jesus steps into the role of Shepherd to the sheep, a scriptural model of leadership which emphasizes the responsibility of human leaders, under God, to care for the sheep, anticipate their needs and provide for them.[1]

The way Jesus sees the crowd governs his response to them, and shapes his relationship with them. He sees them as needing a particular kind of leadership, so he begins to 'teach them many things' (6.34). Presumably, he proclaims the 'good news of God', sets out his vision of the kingdom, perhaps using the image of a feast to which everyone is invited and at which all needs are met. Perhaps he tells stories which explain his strategy and gives examples with which they can identify, so that they can see how this feast of good things applies to them; imagine that they are invited, received, welcomed and honoured; glimpse the awesome truth he wishes to convey: that here, in that 'deserted place' beside the lake, they are heirs to the abundance of God.

If so, this would be only the content of his proclamation. There is also the connection he establishes with his audience, which encourages them to take him seriously. He shows them that he loves them by the way he approaches them. The teacher must respect the audience before the audience will respect the teacher. So Jesus demonstrates his compassion for the crowd, regardless of how he is actually feeling and regardless of the circumstances, because it is the foundation of his character; it shapes his primary relationships with himself and God. His teaching is convincing because he can find that compassion; he shows them what love looks like.

We tend to take Jesus' compassion, and his response to the crowd, for granted. We assume that it was inevitable, that he never had to work at it; we assume he found it easy. But Jesus was human, as we are. Can we take our own compassion for granted? Can we always rely on other people's love, encouragement, affirmation and goodwill? Well, no. So what if Jesus' compassion for the crowd was not automatic? What if he did not find it easy to love them, let alone continue giving of himself when he was tired and hungry? What if he actually shared many of the thoughts and feelings that the apostles were experiencing, but chose not to see the crowd in those terms, not to follow those thoughts or to act on those feelings? What if he chose to act as if he had compassion for them, when perhaps he would much rather have been doing something else?

We should not assume that compassion was his immediate, spontaneous response. Perhaps his generosity emerged from a process – a way of creative thinking – that he went through as the boat came to land and he saw that his plans were wrecked because the crowd had arrived ahead of him. Perhaps compassion was the outcome of his willingness to believe, to have faith, to choose life.

In recounting how Jesus chose to touch a man with leprosy (1.40–42), Mark shows us that the power of God in Jesus operates within the framework of Jesus' context, circumstances and choices. God is present within the creative processes of Jesus' vision, thoughts, attitudes and actions. God acts as Jesus decides. 'I do choose,' he says. 'Be made clean!' It is a defining moment. God's cleansing, healing, renewing grace, poured out upon Jesus at the time of his baptism, is a power with which he must choose to collaborate. He can, if he wills, withhold it.

Jesus is our Shepherd because he chooses to be so. Here, as on every other occasion, he chooses the most positive, creative, life-giving option available. He chooses *life*. He also chooses not to see the crowd as subordinate and weak, but as fellow-pilgrims alongside himself, and full of the same potential. It is as a traveller amongst travellers that he offers them, and us, what he has learned about the 'way'.

It is Jesus' way of envisaging what is there, and of imagining what might be possible, which sets his thinking apart from that of his disciples. This includes the way he sees the disciples themselves. He does not see them as powerless but as his partners. They may believe that they have nothing left to give, but he thinks differently: 'You give them something to eat.' He believes they can. Such is the measure of his faith in them. He believes it because he has taught them the 'way' and he believes that together they can use the 'way' to find everything required.

Admittedly, this is an extreme test; the need is urgent and overwhelming. But it was to learn how to face this depth of hunger – in themselves and in others – that Jesus brought them here in the first place. He wants to take their understanding of the 'way' of faith to another level.

Question: What is my part in ensuring that the need of the multitude is met? Who is responsible for equipping and empowering me to play my part wisely and well? God? The Church? Others? Myself? Or all of these?

Reflection: Deuteronomy 30.15–20. Choose life!

> You choose to make me clean:
> choose to see me,
> choose to hear me,
> choose to touch my wound with tender fingers,
> choose to believe that I am so much more
> than any bruise or burden,
> role or responsibility,
> mask or sin,
> I bear.
>
> You choose to make me clean:
> purified of all that distracts me
> and distorts your lithe intent,
> all that makes me diseased,
> all that defeats the life
> which you are whittling
> to a telling
> point.
>
> You choose to make me whole,
> because wholeness is your aim, your purpose,
> your ideal and dream:
> for me, for us,
> for everyone, without exception.
> Wholeness of body, mind,
> heart, soul and spirit.
> A wholeness

we might not attain
just yet;
might not attain on earth,
but which you carry
in your heart for us.
A cup that brims
with loving possibility,
loving potential,
love.

You choose, so that I can choose:
so that I have a choice;
so that I can choose life;
so that I know
how to make choices
which generate
healing.
You choose,
so that I am
free to choose
and to be chosen.

Free.

Chapter 4
Receiving the Gift

The parcel arrives on Christmas Eve. The courier hands it to me with relief: a rectangular object, about the size of a shoe box. 'I don't know what's in it, love, but it's heavy. What are you expecting?'

'I don't know.' I am puzzled. I heft it in my hands: and yes, he is right, it is heavy – it feels solid and significant. It is well wrapped in strong brown paper and plenty of tape, and clearly addressed to me. I do not recognize the handwriting, nor, when I turn it over, the sender's name and address. 'As far as I know, I'm not expecting anything.'

'Probably a brick then,' he grins, 'Sign here.'

'Just as long as it isn't a bomb,' I say, and we laugh awkwardly, because we know it is no laughing matter at all. I sign the paper he gives me, wish him a Merry Christmas, and shut the door on the cold, damp, day. I was in the middle of decorating the Christmas cake when the doorbell rang so I take the parcel back into the kitchen and set it down on the only part of the work surface that is not smothered in icing sugar. I will examine it later, I tell myself. When I have time.

I finish mixing the royal icing, and spoon it over the cake, spreading it with a knife and then spiking it into little peaks as Delia suggests. It has to be said that the finished result does not very much resemble the drawing in her book, looking instead rather like an upturned bucket that has been left out in a snowstorm, but I reason that once I have added ribbon and a few holly leaves and a plastic Father Christmas, it will be presentable enough, and that by the time we get round to cutting it, everyone will be too full to care anyway. So I put the cake on a tray in the dining-room, away from the cat, the dog, the children, the husband and anyone else who might want to sniff, lick or nibble.

But on my return to the kitchen, I pick up the parcel again. Where has it come from? Who has sent it? What is inside? The sender's name still means nothing. I have never even been to that part of the country. Who is he? How does he know me? What has he sent me?

The trouble is: I really don't have time for this right now. There is still so much to do before my parents arrive back with the children; before my husband gets home from work; before we all sit down for dinner; before we all go out to church. There are presents to wrap. Labels to write. Vegetables to peel. I want to mix the Christmas pudding and prepare it for steaming. I want to make some more mince pies.

For the next hour, I slog on down the list, all the while thinking about the parcel, which sits on the bench like stone in a stream, diverting the current of my attention so that I am unable to give the whole of my mind to anything else.

As a result, I become increasingly muddled and frustrated. In the end, I decide that I won't be able to concentrate until I have solved the puzzle. So I stop in the middle of sifting flour, lay down the sieve, wipe my hands on my apron, and dig my address-book out of a drawer. I am the sort of person who still exchanges Christmas cards with people we met once over dinner while on holiday 25 years ago, so the book is thick and tatty and held together with an elastic band. But though I sift through the addresses of friends, relatives and acquaintances gathered over a lifetime, there is no mention of the person who has sent the parcel. In desperation, I even try directory enquiries, but if he has a number, it is unlisted.

There is nothing else for it. I will have to open it, and it's best to do it now, at once, before the family arrives home to complicate matters with their questions. So I use the kitchen scissors on the tape, and after some intensive snipping, the brown paper comes off. Underneath, there is another layer, a handsome thick red and gold paper. But no note, no label, no explanation.

I am no longer worried, even in the back of my mind, that it might be a bomb. People who send letter-bombs do not waste money on luxury Christmas paper. But I am beginning to wonder if this present is likely to cause a rather different kind of explosion: if this is an elaborate prank, if someone I know has set me up. If so, I must admit that they have me completely fooled. I have no idea who they are, and I have no idea what they have sent me.

I remove the paper – carefully, as it is worth saving – and find that underneath, there is a thick layer of coloured tissue. I take that off as well, and with equal care. Inside there is a beautiful wooden box. The sides glow with polish; the top is fretted, carved, and inlaid in a type of work I have never seen before; the whole box is fragrant with a deep, earthy musk, as if the wood still carries the memory of the living tree. It is exquisite, but I am still baffled. For it is heavy, and the wood itself does not account for the weight of it. What can it contain?

And this is where I am stumped, because though I look very hard, I can find no way to open it. There is no lid, no lock, no visible hinge. I press it all over, gently but also firmly, but cannot find a hidden spring. Smelling it, shaking it and peering at it closely, even with a magnifying glass, produces no further clues. It does not rattle. There is no sense of anything shifting within it. It smells only of the wood itself, and try as I might, I cannot see inside it, even through the fretwork.

I spend a long time trying, only reluctantly putting it away when I hear my parents' car turning into the drive, and the squeals of my children as they run into the porch. Then I hurry to clear away the paper, and to hide the box in a cupboard that is seldom opened because, for some reason that I cannot explain, I do not want anyone else to see it and ask questions about it. It is my box and my mystery. It has been sent to me, and I want to be the person to disclose its secret.

But there is no time to take the box out of its hiding place during the rest of that day, nor the next day nor for many days afterwards. I have to pay attention to each person and each activity while saving some mind-space to think about the next meal. I enjoy it all, as I always do, but at the same time I long for a moment in which I can sit in quiet and recollect myself: gather the scattered pieces of my mind and focus them into something beautiful that is for me and me alone. Everyone wants my time and my energy – where, in the midst of all this busyness, can I find a moment that is just for me?

As this feeling grows, I find myself thinking more and more about the box. I think about it while I am unwrapping my other presents on Christmas Day. I am grateful for everything I receive, and indeed, have chosen many of the gifts myself, so why does my mind keep wandering to the cupboard where the box is hidden and to the box itself: its beauty, its weight, its smell, its mystery, its potential?

What is it about the box that makes me feel dissatisfied – not with what I have, or have given – but rather as if we have missed the point of giving presents at all? I look at the things I have chosen for myself and wonder why they are all so ordinary. Unexciting. Useful. Practical. Dull. I look at what I have given other people, and wonder whether anything I give could ever stimulate in them the unexplained, unexplored, unlimited longing that this mysterious, unopened box has awakened in me . . .

To be continued

The gesture of acceptance

The first step in Jesus' strategy for making the vision of the kingdom into an experience of the kingdom is summed up and symbolized by the way he takes the bread into his hands.

It shows us how he 'receives what is given'. The 'givens' in this situation are the crowd, the disciples, himself, the challenge that faces them, the environment around them and resources available to meet the need. As Jesus talks with his disciples, most of the 'givens' are clear to him. The one unknown is the amount of food that the disciples can actually lay their hands on. So he sends them to investigate (6.38). It takes their minds off their anxieties, which are beginning to inflate into alarm, and it focuses their attention on what they actually have, rather than on what they do not have.

We can see the value of Jesus' reaction more clearly if we consider what he did not do. He could have denied that there was a problem, dithered or refused to take a decision, on the grounds that he did not know what to do, or that it was nothing to do with him. He could have avoided the issue entirely by leaving the scene. He could have criticized the disciples for becoming inordinately anxious or made them feel small for interrupting him. He could have preached against gluttony or given a lesson on the spiritual significance of fasting. He could have become angry and frustrated that such mundane matters were distracting their attention from his important work, or blamed the crowd for being poorly prepared, or the disciples for not warning him sooner. He could have asked questions like 'Why me?' or 'Why now?' or declared, 'It's not fair!' He could have bemoaned the state of the economy or ranted against the rich, or launched a scorching attack on Jews who sucked their compatriots dry by collaborating with Rome.

These are all normal human reactions to adversity, anxiety and tension. The fact that Jesus did not react like this demonstrates his profound acceptance of the situation as it is. He is willing to accept – to receive – what is given.

We can receive what is given even if it is not what we need or what we would have wanted for ourselves, or for others. We can accept a situation without liking it, condoning it, or indeed believing it to be desirable at all. We can accept that this is where we are; this is the situation we are in. Similarly, to accept the resources we are given does not necessarily mean that we have to regard them as adequate or appropriate or complete. All it means is that we recognize that this is what we have been given to work with.

This is complex acceptance: an attitude in which we accept a situation because we are confident we can work with it to create something better. We accept the people around us because we are all travellers together, heading in the same general direction. We accept the resources we have to hand because we are confident we can use them to generate what we need. We accept ourselves because after every mistake or failing, we get back on the road.

The strategy of faith begins with this attitude of complex or intentional acceptance. Whatever our opinion or our feelings, we accept the 'givens' because it is our intention to work with them in a positive, creative manner. We factor the 'way' into the equation. 'Where we are' is the beginning of a process.

Jesus' responses that day consistently signal this profound, complex, intentional acceptance. He accepts the presence of the crowd, even though he wanted to be alone with the apostles. He accepts the crowd's need for a particular kind of leadership, and the task of providing what they need, whether or not this is what he would have chosen for himself. He accepts the disciples as his partners in mission, even though they feel incapable of helping him. He accepts the moment, even though the hour is late and he is almost certainly tired. He accepts the challenge – to provide food for the whole company – even though the company is so large. And he accepts the resources he is given to work with, even though they are not enough to feed so many.

Jesus' whole attitude of profound, complex, intentional acceptance is summed up and symbolized in the simple gesture of taking the bread and fish into his hands. It is impossible to overstate the significance of this action. In doing this, he demonstrates that however the situation has arisen, he intends to deal with it. However great or powerful the chaos that swirls around him, he knows what he is doing, or, to put it another way, he knows what God can do and how he can collaborate with that process. However inadequate the resources, he intends to work with them until they meet the need of the multitude.

What is happening here? This is the action of a fool – for it makes no sense at all. This is the action of a cynic – for how can he expect us to believe that such a tiny quantity of food can feed so many? This is the action of a conjuror, a magician – isn't he manipulating the way we see things, the way we think and respond? This is an actor stepping into a role, inviting us to suspend our disbelief, engaging us in a game of 'let's pretend'. This is Jesus of Nazareth, the Son of Man, the Christ, showing us an alternative reality and encouraging us to act as if it is true.

What is happening here? The answer to that depends on what you see, and that in turn depends on how you have been taught to see the world and the people in it, and the extent to which you have challenged, adapted and amended the way you have learned to see. What is happening here? Choose a viewpoint, and that viewpoint will determine what happens next.

Question: What are the 'givens' in my situation, here and now? Can I 'receive' them with the intention of working with them in a positive, creative manner?

Reflection: Psalm 11. How can I run away? It is here that I live. It is here that God helps me.

Taking the bread into our hands,
we hold the moment
and all that it contains,
for good and ill:
the place in which we are set,

the people, as they are,
the resources given,
even though they are not enough.

Taking the moment into our hands,
we choose:
whether we react or respond,
whether we will rise to this challenge,
how we survey our options,
whether we will take the one which best fits
the purpose of God.

Taking the choice into our hands,
we turn towards the task:
the thing that only we can do,
the thing that only God can do,
the thing which must happen
if we are to cross the divide
between need and contentment,
hunger, and the bread that satisfies.

Taking the task into our hands,
we accept the risk of this Way:
the folly of those who walk this road,
choosing life, creating renewal,
earthing the impossible,
till kingdom come.

Creating space to change

The tray was full of bits and pieces: coloured card, scraps of felt, lengths of ribbon, snippets from various kinds of plastic used in packaging, and the kind of foil that seals a tub of margarine. Some of the bits the artist would use at once: she could see how they would fit into the design she was creating. Others had potential: she liked them for their shape, colour or texture, and though she could not see at present how they would complement the other elements, she was willing to work with them until they found their place.

But there were some scraps which would only ever be included after a great deal of effort. She had washed them, shaped them, smoothed them out. She had looked at them from different angles, and sorted them into different combinations and still they seemed to exist at a tangent to everything else. In a sense, they were the most exciting pieces of all; experience had taught her that one of these bits, in just the right spot, would bring the work alive. But it might take years of patient endeavour to find that spot and in the meantime, the bits stayed on the tray, apparently useless, going nowhere; but she kept them, mainly because she never, ever threw anything away.

Jesus' attitude to others is a similar kind of 'complex acceptance': a willingness to meet the crowd where he finds them and work with them until they experience the fullness of life he believes God wants them to receive. His problem is that when he meets them, they are not where he wants them to be. Something will have to change before he can satisfy their hunger. He cannot produce food for about 5,000 people unless something happens to change the resources, the people or their circumstances. And whatever the nature of the change, the people themselves will have to be prepared to participate in it or at the very least accept it, so that they can benefit from it.

In other words, whatever happens, Jesus needs the crowd to 'move on' psychologically and spiritually – to learn to see, think and act differently. However, this requires energy: to receive a new thing, to contemplate how it will change our world, and to consider the response that it requires. Much of the time, we do not have enough energy for this, even if it will be good for us; so we develop habits, patterns, routines and customs and use them to conserve our limited resources. When we are tired or worn down, our routines comfort us; not just because they are familiar, but because they allow us to use our limited amount of energy where it is needed most.

Jesus needs the crowd to 'move on', but he sees that is precisely what they are unable to do. Does he blame them for this? No, he accepts this as a 'given', and gets the people to sit down. In other words, he signals that they do not have to take responsibility, fend for themselves, worry about one another, or become anxious about what will happen. As their shepherd, he is taking charge.

This is the reassurance they need. They do not feel capable of movement, not through obstinacy or sinfulness but simply because they are hungry, weary, sick and burdened; they do not know which way to turn; and they are afraid. They fear their frailty because it makes them vulnerable; if dispersed, they will become divided into those who can fend for themselves, and those who cannot. In any search for food, the young and fit and those with means will be pitted against the elderly, sick and poor, with the probable result that the weakest will get nothing at all.

Jesus' order helps them to feel safe, because it demonstrates that he knows their need and is taking it into account. It is encouraging, because it suggests that they are staying put and staying together; that all will be included, even the most fragile; and that the necessary, life-giving change will not demand of them – any of them – more than they can give.

As they have been reassured on all these important points, they are able to use their limited energy to adjust to the possibility of change. Jesus has created a 'breathing space' in which they are free to consider an alternative future; and because they are not yet committed to any particular course of action, they are free to choose whether or not they get involved in whatever he is about to do.

People are much more likely to change if they are given this positive mix of security and freedom. They are more willing to take risks if they can start from a place of safety, or to go in a new direction if they are allowed to start from a place that feels familiar, or reasonably comfortable. And they will go further and faster in a challenging venture if they are able to keep their options open as the situation begins to move around them. This is because people become ready to commit to a process at different stages and for different reasons. Some are in from the first moment, while others need to travel alongside for a time, feeling their way, seeing how things go, gaining confidence in the leader, in one another, the project and themselves. Paradoxically, by implying that the people do not have to move in one particular way, Jesus makes it possible for them to 'move on' in other ways – in this case, psychologically and spiritually.

The 'breathing space' is the place where God breathes into us the life we need to go forward. One way in which this happens is by freeing up, gathering and focusing the energy we already possess. Part of this energy resides in our emotions – the expression of our energy, our vitality, our life. A truly honest acceptance of the 'givens' of a situation must include accepting how we feel about it. Unless we are able to recognize our emotions and willing to accept that they are a powerful factor in any context, they are likely to distort the way we see, think and act. This can be catastrophic for the creative process: not just because unacknowledged emotions can then limit, damage or even destroy the good we do, but also because our emotions contain the very energy we need to harness for God's purposes. We recognize and address our emotions so that all our energies and powers can be channelled into the good and glorious thing that God is doing in our midst.

Jesus anticipates the emotions aroused by the event. He accepts that these emotions are part of the situation and that he must make allowances for them. Further, he knows that he can use them, and therefore the strength of feeling amongst the crowd is channelled in a positive direction. It takes everyone forward, and it moves them on together.

The 'breathing space' may not happen automatically. Most of the time, such spaces have to be created. Mark's comment that the people sat down in groups of hundreds and of fifties (6.40), reminds us that a degree of organization is often required to create this kind of 'space' in a situation. Of course, it was because they were excellent at organization that the Romans were able to conquer and govern much of the known world. In this case, however, people are not being coerced into change. Rather, the way they are organized gives them the freedom to consider change, secure in the knowledge that no one is committed to anything, that no costly, irrevocable decisions have yet been taken.

God does not force us to move, but instead gives us a place of safety in which we can pause, reflect and choose how to respond to the challenges before us. We can see our options as possibilities, some of which might have potential. We can muster all our different forms of energy, and see that we have been given the freedom and the power to make our own decision. We can sense that others are ready to move forward with us. We can become engaged of our own free will, and with the whole of ourselves, moving forward because we this is what we want to do.

Question: Where do I need to create a 'breathing space' to help me deal with a process of change? How can this be organized so that there is an adequate opportunity to 'breathe' before moving on?

Reflection: Genesis 2.4–9. The breath of God creates a living being.

Received, known,
welcomed, valued:
here is an eternal invitation,
to re-connect with One
who is utterly alive;
to re-enter the experience
of being absolutely loved.

God is with us.
Any glimpse we may have
of compassion or kindness,
goodness or generosity,
harmony or hope,
is but a glimmer of the wealth
God holds.
For us. For me. For you.
The moment might be fleeting,
but the glory is forever;
always present;
always available;

always accessible;
always now.

Here in the sacred space
we re-enter the truth of this,
recall it to mind,
and let ourselves
be here,
breathe here,
where God breathes into us
the air that makes us vital,
the air that makes us able
to bring life
into the world.

Receiving the child

We are made for a life that reflects the life of God: creative, expansive, productive, self-replicating and fulfilling. This is our inheritance as human beings. If we have a distinction as Christians, it is that we know how to realize this promise. We can act as if it is true. Thanks to Jesus, we can imagine abundance and make it specific, concrete, personal and real. He has shown us how to unpack the mystery parcel, reveal the gift and release the potential found within.

When Jesus described this process, he spoke of 'receiving' the kingdom like a child (10.13–16). Children are our examples because they see the world with fresh eyes. They live in the now – they are curious, questioning, open-minded and open-hearted, lacking our adult assumptions about what is realistic and reliable. They become totally absorbed in whatever is right before them. They feel free to play, experiment, explore, enjoy. They are willing to use their imaginations, their instincts and their intuition. They regard questions like 'Why?' 'Why not?' and 'What if?' as doorways into alternative worlds and will happily act as if those worlds exist. They wonder. They trust. They believe.

Jesus warns us that unless we have this receptive 'childlike' attitude, we will never enter the kingdom at all. He invites us to rediscover in ourselves a childlike way of seeing, thinking, feeling and acting, as the foundation of our ability to love, hope and trust; so that we can have faith and keep faith. He offers us the key to the kingdom.

Unfortunately, we adults are so often reluctant to 'receive' the child: both the child in our midst, and the child within ourselves. Frequently, this is because we were not 'received' ourselves when we were children. Perhaps we were always being told that 'children should be seen and not heard'. Perhaps we were always in the way, or always hustled out whenever anything important was happening or excluded from significant discussions. Perhaps we were always being told that it is rude to interrupt; that good children only speak when they are spoken to. Perhaps we never felt that our conversation was valued, that our ideas were worth a hearing, that our ambitions were approved or that our talents were taken seriously.

If we have been belittled or diminished as children, then as we grow up we can find it particularly difficult to 'receive' children ourselves, including that part of us which remains a child. No one has ever shown us how a child can be 'received' in the adult world, or how adults can value and affirm the contribution of the child. As a result, we may resist 'childish' things, even reject them entirely, without recognizing that by doing so we are denying or distorting a strong and vital aspect of ourselves, which forms the foundation of our ability to see, think and act with faith, hope and love.

Our ability to function in a 'childlike' manner is that part of ourselves which allows us to remain young at heart, vibrant and vital, however old we become; that part of ourselves which is still experimenting, learning, growing and blooming; that aspect of ourselves which enables us to receive life in all its fullness and give life to others.

In our society, the desire to 'give life' to someone else is often expressed in the cards we send and the gifts we give. We give gifts when we want to celebrate life – to mark birthdays and anniversaries, at weddings and christenings, on retirement – and when we want to reaffirm life in the face of death, as at times of sickness, anxiety or mourning. The cards we send bear images of life, fruitfulness, fullness, feasting, plenty, leisure or luxury; in other words, we send them to help someone 'imagine abundance'. Similarly, the gifts we give – flowers, fruit, chocolate, useful items or luxury goods – symbolize the 'more life' that we want for those we respect or love; the 'abundance' we would give them if we could.

Just as a child is able to play, experiment and explore, so the child in us is able to 'imagine abundance' – for ourselves and for those around us – and it is this facility which allows us to be creative in many other ways. When we 'imagine abundance' we are seeing, thinking and acting like a child. We are venturing out in faith, hope and love. In so doing, we receive life and share it. We can 'unpack' the gift of life which we have been given, invest it in a way which causes it to grow, and distribute it so that life is more generally available. This is how we fulfil our potential as the children of God, made in the divine image, partners with God in the creation of abundant life for all.

If, in the course of our own childhood, we rarely felt 'received', we tend to play down the importance of knowing that we are seen, heard, valued and respected, however small and weak we may be, however 'childlike' our contribution to the moment. We may even have convinced ourselves that as adults we have put away 'childish things'. But how can we put away something we have never actually known, held, experienced? In truth, the way of our healing is to recognize that Jesus can show us what we have missed. Jesus shows us how God receives us: the child we were and that part of ourselves which will always be 'childlike', and which retains this essential capacity to see and think and feel and act like a child.

In all creation, only human beings are made in the image of God. We are welcomed by God as a reflection of the Godself, because God sees the divine likeness in us. No sin, however terrible, obscures this image entirely or forever. This is the hope, the sorrow, the pain and the grace of God: that however damaged we are, however badly we damage ourselves or other people, God can still see the divine likeness in us. And Jesus makes this real by receiving us with smiling eyes, open arms, a welcoming lap. He offers the hospitality of the heart, his willingness to embrace, listen, get involved, play, bless.

This is how we are received by God: with this kind of loving attention. God sees us as well worth seeing, hearing and listening to. God wants to spend time with us and get involved with us. God values our company and values us by paying attention to our needs, our concerns, our desires. God invests in us because God considers us worth the investment. This is how God views you and me. Not as objects of pity. Not as victims or sufferers. Not as pathetic, weak, inadequate individuals. And certainly not as miserable sinners.

God receives us as a gift.

Do you have any good memories of receiving a gift when you were a child? Did you ever receive something that made you feel surprised, intrigued, excited, grateful, wonderful, beloved? Did you ever enjoy the fun of guessing what the parcel might contain, and then discovering that it was something even better than you had imagined?

We value gifts because they are given as symbols of abundance; in particular because they express the abundant life that someone wants us to enjoy. It is when the gift does not enable us to imagine abundance for ourselves – or when it is given in a manner which robs the experience of its full pleasure – that we feel disappointed, embarrassed or dismayed by the presents we are given. The ideal gift is a form of 'abundance' – especially 'abundant life' – or else it is something which makes abundance possible, something which allows us to find or create or experience it, something which takes us a step closer to our heart's desire. The best 'givers' are those who enable us to discover the plenty that is available to us, including he potential that is within us. Can you imagine God receiving you as a gift? A gift that God unfolds with wonder and delight? Jesus invites us to see ourselves like this; to see others like this; to see the world like this: as if everything is resonant with life and light.

Question: How was I received as a child? What did this teach me? Do I need to unlearn some of these lessons so that I can grow in wonder and delight?

Reflection: 1 Samuel 3. The child as a trustworthy prophet of the Lord.

> I do not have do it all,
> I do not have to do it all at once,
> I do not have to do it all perfectly,
> I do not have to do it alone:
> because here and now, as I do what I can,
> you love me.
>
> I do not have to be good all the time,
> I do not have to be right all the time,
> I do not have to be enough,
> I do not have to be holy:
> because here and now, as I am who I am,
> you love me.
>
> When I fail, fall down, let myself down,
> let others down, you still see me as more
> than my failure, more
> than all the things I have neglected to do,
> more than all the things I have done wrong,
> more than the worst thing
> I have ever done.
>
> You love me.
> I do not understand this love,
> I do not understand it at all:
> how you can do this;
> how you can love like this;
> how you can love me like this;
> how you can hold for me a love
> that is steadfast, unconquerable,
> unchanging, indestructible,
> infinite, eternal.

I will never understand it,
but I can accept it,
grateful that it is so;
I can allow it to make a difference,
because it does indeed
make a difference.
It frees me to gaze, wonder,
elaborate, experiment.
It means that sometimes
I can let myself off the hook,
cut myself some slack,
give myself some credit,
enjoy what I have achieved.
It enables me to relax
and let you go on loving:
loving me;
loving those I love;
loving those around me,
whether or not I love them
as they deserve;
loving the world.

And then, as I let you love me,
there are those moments
when I find myself
startled into play.

Living in the now

Children live in the now. Whatever a child sees, wants or does is always immediate, this minute. Children remind us that the present moment is where we live. Life is transient. Life is dynamic. Our existence is not static but fluid, constantly on the move as each moment opens, passes, closes. As individuals, we bob along on personal currents that mingle, separate, alter direction, then mingle again, only to part company once more. Our personal current is made up of moments of time in which we live. We live in an ever-present now.

In a sense, the present moment – and all it contains – is all we ever have. We may be able to remember the past, but we do not live there. We cannot take action there or change what happened there. The past is done and finished. It remains with us in many ways: in memory and all its associations; in our education; in our skills and experience. It has marked us physically, emotionally, psychologically and spiritually. It has formed us. But it has moved out of our reach.

Similarly, the future is not yet ours, and it never will be. We can plan for it and anticipate it, but we cannot control it. We cannot live there, because it is not yet with us. We can use our imaginations to project ourselves into it, but by the time it arrives, it is the present, and however we may have imagined it, it looks different. We do not know what will happen in the future. We can guess, but even our most educated guess is not the same as the knowledge we can have of the now.

The present moment is all we have. So the present moment is where we see, think, plan and work. And we have work to do. However few our moments might be, they are always enough to make a beginning. We can begin where we are, as we are and with what we have, however inadequate our resources may be. It is never too soon – or too late – to make a beginning. We do not have to wait until we achieve a particular age, level of energy, experience, or expertise. Nor need we despair if the optimum moment has passed us by. Beginning is for anyone, anywhere, at any time, facing anything. It is always worth making a beginning – it is always worth making a good beginning – because it is the foundation of everything else.

My maternal grandmother used to say: 'If you look after the pennies, the pounds will look after themselves.' Individual moments are fleeting, but they add up, so that, if we use our minutes rather than wasting them, we may discover an hour we did not know we had.

Moreover, by paying attention to the present moment, we become present to the moment, able to notice, explore, appreciate and absorb far more of what it contains. Any one moment contains more than we can see. We cannot create time, but we can learn to pay more attention to what is happening within us and around us, to be 'present' to life, and so live it to the full. By paying attention to the present moment we live wholly in it, and we discover that the present moment can expand. The more we practise being present to the moment, the more we discover just how 'large' a moment can be.

When we are utterly absorbed in something we enjoy doing, the experience fills us and we inhabit time in a manner which both magnifies our satisfaction and the creative potential of our activity. We are fed, and we create something which can feed others as well. By paying attention to the moment, we become more securely rooted in all that is real and true: in ourselves, in our context, and in God.

The more we practise being present to the moment, the more we learn how to pay attention, with all that we are. We learn to notice what is happening around us and within us, not only using our senses, or our rational minds, but using our emotions, imaginations, memory, will and spirit, too. We become more aware in all these different ways, able to recognize the information we are being given, analyse it, decide what is useful and deploy it as necessary.

And as we do so, we find that the moment magnifies exponentially, because we are paying attention to many aspects of ourselves, all at the same time.

The Revd Sister Mary Holliday used to speak of 'moments that take a lot of unpacking'. Any and every moment can be like this. Like Dr Who's TARDIS, the present moment is larger on the inside than it may seem on the outside. It is a door that opens into a much larger space. It is a portal into the vast reaches of space and time. It is a crack which gives us a glimpse into eternity.

Question: What is going on around me and within me at the moment? What are my senses (sight, hearing, smell, taste, touch) telling me? What are memory, reason and imagination saying? What do I want to happen? How is God loving me in this moment?

Reflection: Lamentations 3.19–33. In the midst of grief, the prophet sits in silence: remembering, waiting, hoping, bearing, suffering, trusting.

Open the door on a new day.
Open the door,
and let the light stream in,
with the draughts and the doubts and the rain in the air,
all that the winter's day brings.
Open the door.
Don't close it, don't bang it shut!
Don't shut me out, God says,
don't shut me out!
I am here, I am with you.
I have come to stay with you.

So open the door on the day
with the troubles and dreams that flood in,
don't resist them.
We'll see what they bring,
together we'll see what they bring
as we walk hand in hand
through the door of the day,
through the door everyday,
together.[1]

God meets us here

The present moment is where God meets us. Now is where we live, act, relate to others. Now is where we connect with God, and God connects with us. 'Seek the Lord while he may be found, call upon him while he is near,' urged the prophet (Isaiah 55.6), not because God is otherwise absent, but because unless we are 'present' when God is ready to meet with us, God cannot show us new things, give us new life, make anything happen through us. God uses the past to teach us and the future to inspire us, but it is in the here and now that God meets us; because it is here and now that the universe of space and time intersects with eternity.

Here and now, God comes to us. Here and now, we approach God. Here and now I can have a relationship with Jesus. Here and now, I am 'in Christ' or 'in the Spirit'. This connection is only possible in the present moment, but it is possible in any and every moment. The present moment is 'a space marked out for God's purposes'; where we can return to the Source; God who meets us in the depths of our hearts, in our encounters with one another, in our engagement with the world.

Question: What do I have 'in my hands' here and now?

Answering this question focuses our attention in the present moment. The issue is not what we had in the past, nor what we would like to have in the future, but only what we have in our hands at this moment. And it is a question worth considering: wherever I am, whatever I am doing, whatever I am facing. If I take the time to be thorough in addressing this question, I may be surprised at how much – and what a variety of material – I 'hold'.

The 'resources' take so many forms. Physical circumstances. Material possessions. Relationships, connections and networks. Gifts, skills, and talents. My participation in events, experiences and employment. Voluntary work. Hobbies, pastimes and cultural interests. Achievements and attainments. Dreams and desires. Vocation. I answer the question as a whole person, living in a multi-dimensional web of association, activity and exchange.

What do we have 'in our hands' here and now? It is worth asking this question of any group facing a significant challenge, especially amongst people who are considered poor, few, elderly, inadequate, helpless and hopeless. Answering this question, even the smallest group can discover 'buried treasure', abilities which have never been recognized before, assets which are held in common, or helpful connections which might yet contribute to the cause.

It is heartening to discover that we have more resources than we thought we had. Of course, some may not be relevant or helpful in facing our current challenge, but we list them anyway, because at this stage we do not really know what will be useful and what will not. We set aside our assumptions. We acknowledge everything available. We include things rather than discounting them. We allow ourselves to look with fresh eyes, so that we can see things as a child might see them. As Jesus sees them.

This is the attitude of the child, for whom the wrapping paper and the ribbon and the cardboard box are as much part of the present as the toy inside it. The adult feels aggrieved that the child spends time playing with the packaging rather than the toy which cost so much money, but the child sees, thinks and behaves in a different way. The child understands that every part of the parcel is gift. It is all given to be examined and explored. It all has value. It all has potential.

Admittedly, some of it has potential we do not know how to use, or which we do not examine because it is too large, or too painful, or too personal to contemplate. When, in 2001, I was diagnosed with breast cancer at the age of 43, some people tried to comfort me with the thought that as a minister and as a writer, I would be able to use the experience to help others. While I appreciated the thought, the truth is that even now, six years later, I do not want to revisit that period, because the memory of undergoing treatment is fused with two other bereavements I experienced at the same time. So, yes, I am investing time and energy in holding that part of my life before God in prayer, but I won't be counselling cancer sufferers or visiting cancer self-help groups for a long time yet, if indeed I ever do. Because some experiences never do turn out to be 'useful'. They defy and deny any sense of purpose. They can only be held as naked pain.

Nevertheless, every part of our experience is gift, including the parts we cannot contemplate and the parts about which we cannot speak. Their potency is hidden from us, or feels as if it can only ever be destructive, but that does not matter providing we are willing to own them and be honest about them, rather than pretend that they do not exist. If we know they are there, and if we are willing to acknowledge that they are part of what we hold in our hands, then whether or not we know how to frame our thoughts in words, they are brought into the 'sacred space' of the present moment.

And this is the place where God meets us. This is where God lives with us, and we live with God: in the 'now', with all that the moment contains, seen and unseen. Here and now, our 'givens' are placed on the table, where God looks at them with us. Each is given to be examined and explored. Each has its value, and its power. We begin to see that perhaps God is helping us to hold it all, that perhaps, in ways we cannot see, what we hold is being converted, healed, transformed.

We glimpse this, but we cannot be sure. We can only stay with what we hold in our hands, in this given moment. And trust.

In doing so, we find that we have opened our hands, our hearts and our minds to all that is true and real in ourselves, in others, in the world and in God. We are touching the rock.

Reflection: Isaiah 55.6–9. Seek, call, return. God is here (now, in the present moment) and God will lead us beyond ourselves.

> Here and now,
> where I am,
> in this moment, this location,
> this particular mental space,
> I am here,
> and Jesus is with me,
> Son of the Father,
> Spirit with my spirit:
> his hope holding mine.
>
> Here and now,
> where I am,
> he speaks, I listen,
> he gives, I receive,
> he waits, I ask,
> he offers, I welcome,
> he invites, I answer,
> his love holding mine.
>
> Here and now,
> where I am,
> with what I am holding,
> with those around me,
> with all that I am,
> with all that I am facing,
> with all you hold in heaven for me,
> even me, I am ready,
> your faith holding mine.

Looking at what we hold

Once we can see what we are holding, we must decide how we are going to look at it. There is a danger that we will miss out this stage because we do not understand its importance. So often, we leap straight from 'What do we have?' to 'What are we going to do with what we have?' or 'What is it possible to do with what we have?'

Some of us jump from discussion to doing because we are hands-on, practical people and we do our best thinking when we are in action. This is fine, providing that our thinking is properly grounded and we are, in fact, ready to act. However, we can be tempted to make this jump too soon, simply through impatience, which is a form of fear. We can rush into action because we fear that unless we act soon, we will be unable to act at all. We can want to see an end product because we fear that unless we see results quickly, there will be no beneficial outcome at all. We are afraid of wasting our time and ending up no better off than we were before.

Pausing to ask ourselves how we are seeing our resources allows us to become aware of the choices we are making. It enables us to be sure that we are seeing – and therefore taking into account – all the available options. This is particularly important when resources are in short supply, when we are under pressure to use what we have wisely and well, especially if – as is often the case – our resources are much smaller than the need.

Question: Is the cup half-empty, or half-full?

Yes, I know the question has become a cliché, but it is still worth asking. There is no 'right' or 'wrong' answer. Rather, what matters is that we notice how we answer it, because that gut reaction is giving us useful information about how we see the situation. If we always tend to react in a similar way, then noticing this gives us useful information about the way example, experience and education have trained our minds to work.

Knowing how I tend to see things allows me to examine my reactions, reflect upon and evaluate them. It enables me to ask whether I could respond more positively, more generously, more compassionately, more creatively. Watching myself respond to the world, to other people and to God does at least open up the possibility that I can alter my vision if I wish; or if doing so will make my work and engagement more effective – closer to what Jesus might have done – a more intimate collaboration with the Spirit of life, joy, justice and hope.

What we 'see' – either with our eyes or in our mind's eye – sets in motion a train of thought laden with assumptions. For example: which way of seeing the situation is the more accurate? Which way of seeing the situation is the more realistic? One assumption leads to another. Small assumptions can lead to much larger ones, all in less time than it takes to blink an eye. Our assumptions build into an attitude, and this hidden train of thought influences – even determines – the way we think, feel, and act.

Is the cup half-empty or half-full? How do I tend to see it? In one sense, it does not matter how we answer, because the two phrases have roughly the same meaning. But if we assume that our way of seeing the situation is the only accurate and realistic way of seeing it – that this is the way the world is and that these are the facts of the situation – then we will react accordingly. We may expect other people to see the situation in the same way, and argue with them if they do not. We may impose that view of the situation on circumstances and events as they develop, and become bewildered, angry and defensive if something occurs which does not fit the picture. We will make decisions about what we can or cannot do with the resources available – whether we feel able to claim them and develop them, use them, share them or give them away – and those decisions will shape our lives, our worship, our relationships, our work and our mission.

Is the cup half-empty or half-full? We might, with some justification, say that the answer does not matter. As a question considered by itself, removed from any context, we might indeed argue this. In our day-to-day existence, however, the question is embedded in circumstances and encounters where our willingness and ability to act, and the nature of our action, could make a significant difference to us and those around us. Which way of seeing the situation will encourage you to take a drink if you are thirsty, or encourage you to offer the glass to someone else who is thirsty?

Suppose, for a moment, that there is a way of seeing things which makes us better able to fulfil the mission that Jesus has given us. If that is so, then the way we look at everything matters enormously. Our perception becomes crucial, because how we tend to see situations, encounters, people, and resources will influence – even determine – our ability to work well with the life-giving elements around us.

If we see the cup as half-empty, we are focusing on the empty space, on what we do not have. Seeing our 'lack' tends to make us think we are inadequate or that the situation is hopeless; it tends to increase our anxiety because we feel that we do not have the resources to do what needs to be done, or to do anything at all. We feel unable to act creatively, and therefore we can feel frustrated, angry, powerless and afraid. We are more likely to believe that we are alone, that we have been let down, betrayed, abandoned.

However, if we see the cup as half-full, the dynamic operates in the opposite direction. We focus on what is present, on what is actually there. We have something 'in our hands'. Yes, we recognize that it is not, in itself, enough, but we choose to stay focused on what we have, rather than becoming distracted by what we do not have. The more we stay focused on what we have, the more we are likely to think about what we can do with it, to feel grateful, resourceful, capable and generous. We are more likely to believe that we can be creative with what we have; that we can use it, risk it, share it with others or even give it to someone else.

So if we want to be more creative more of the time, seeing the cup as 'half-full' gives us an in-built advantage. If we have not been trained to think like this, then the challenge is to examine and explore the way we see, think, believe and behave so that we learn how to see things in this positive manner.

If there is a more creative way of looking at things, am I willing to consider it? It is not that other ways of seeing the world are necessarily wrong or inaccurate, but rather that this particular way enables us to make the most of whatever becomes available. It helps us see the life that is present, and encourages us to work with it until it begins to grow. This way of seeing and thinking fosters faith, and a life of faith. It allows us to take opportunities, explore new avenues, consider other courses of action. We become excited by potential and what we can do to bring it to fulfilment.

Reflection: 2 Kings 6.15–17. Two views of the same situation.

Call me beyond my knowledge:
to trust in your faithfulness,
to rely on your love,
to bear witness to your attentive grace;
to offer you my all.

Call us beyond our understanding:
so that we are rooted in your reality,
so that we bud and blossom and bear fruit,
so that we share your harvest.

Call nations beyond their experience:
as you fill us with your life,
as you fulfil our dreams of abundance,
as you draw us closer to one another and to you,
as you let your peace well up,
your joy flow out.

God's glory revealed in me.
God's glory revealed in us.
God's glory revealed in all creation.

Chapter 5
The Art of Abundance

Continued from chapter 4. . . .

Several days after Christmas, when my parents have gone home, my husband has gone back to work, and the children have gone back to school, I get a phone call. A male voice that I do not recognize calls me by name in a tone that is friendly but not over-familiar. At first, I assume that he is trying to sell me something, and I am about to launch into my refusal when he asks: 'Did you receive the box?'

'Who is this?' I ask.

'Oh, you don't know me,' he says. 'And please, there is no reason to be anxious. I'm just the person who sent you the box. As they say, I saw it and thought of you. Did you receive it?'

'Yes, I did.'

'And has it opened for you yet?'

'Er . . . no. I couldn't work out how to open it.'

'You don't need to. It will open of its own accord,' he said. 'Just think about it, and what it means to you, and eventually, it will open for you.'

Excuse me? How does that work, exactly? But for some reason, I don't like to ask, so instead: 'What's in it?'

'Treasure.'

Yes, of course. 'What kind of treasure?'

'What kind of treasure do you want?'

'I don't know.'

'Ah well, that is something to think about then, isn't it? You keep asking yourself that question, and the box will soon open for you.'

'But how is that going to work? If I don't know what I want, how can anyone else know?'

'Quite.'

'So how can the treasure in the box be something I want?'

'Oh, I'm not going to tell you how the box works. I just know that if you keep on thinking about what really matters to you, what really excites you and interests you and motivates you or, to put it another way, if you clarify the shape of your treasure and your heart's desire – and pay some attention to it – then the box will open. And you will find what you are seeking. That's all.'

I don't know what to say. So I say nothing.

'Do you believe me?' he asks, after a pause.

'I don't think I do,' I tell him. 'But I've got the box, and it's solid enough, and it's also quite heavy, so there must be something in it. I guess I have to believe you. A little bit, anyway.'

'That's fine. That's great,' he said, 'I think you'll find that little bit is all you need.'

'If you say so.'

'I do say so,' he laughs. 'And will you do as I ask? Pay attention to your heart's desire?'

'Sure,' I tell him, because by now I am wondering what sort of weirdo I am talking to, and how I might get rid of him. 'I'll do that. Once I've worked out what it is.'

'That's good,' he says. 'That's the spirit. Do that, and the box will open in no time. Happy New Year.' And he rings off.

I take the box out of its hiding-place and look at it. I still cannot see how it might open, but it is solid, and beautiful, and real, and somehow undeniably there. Or rather, *here*. Here with me. Here in my life. Part of my existence. I am beginning to think that I will have to take it seriously. Somehow. When I have worked out what my treasure is. And how I can pay attention to it.

The thought of doing that is actually rather daunting. I mean, it's exciting, yes. Definitely. But also rather scary. You see, I've always assumed that finding treasure was complicated, difficult, even dangerous. A task for heroes. Not ordinary people like me. And shouldn't I have a map or a wise old guide or some clues or a set of instructions? Surely it can't be – well – simple. Can it? So yes, while it is all very exciting and intriguing and even inspiring in some ways, it is also rather more than I can think about at the moment, in the midst of everything else that is going on. Tomorrow, perhaps. Yes, I will definitely think about it tomorrow.

Or the day after.

The gesture of gratitude

If the first move in Jesus' strategy is to take the bread into his hands – to receive what is given – then his second move is to pray. Once again, it is worth asking the obvious questions. Why does he pray? What form does his prayer take? What does it express? And what difference does it make, that he prays with the bread in his hands?

Jesus 'looked up to heaven, and blessed . . . the loaves' (6.41). What was this 'blessing'? What does Mark believe Jesus was doing? How might Jesus have understood this action himself?

The word Mark uses is '*eulogeo*', which the NRSV translates as 'blessing' several other times in his Gospel. For example, in the story of the feeding of the four thousand, he writes of Jesus blessing the fish (8.7), and at the Last Supper, Jesus blesses the bread (14.22). The key to Mark's use of the word comes when Jesus is brought before the chief priests, elders and scribes and the high priest asks him: 'Are you the Messiah, the Son of the Blessed One?' (14.61). His answer, 'I am', is interpreted as blasphemous, even though it is carefully qualified with a reference to Daniel's vision of one who receives his authority from God. For Mark, Jesus' blessing of the bread, which leads to his meeting a multitude of need, demonstrates Jesus' closeness to God, the Source of life. However Jesus' dignity or status are defined, he 'comes in the name of the Lord' (11.9); speaking the life-giving word. His blessings carry God's power to generate, magnify and transform life. Those willing to become like children can recognize this (10.15), enter the kingdom and feast at God's table.

However, to the Jewish mind, God is so awesome, so holy, so Other, that any person claiming a particular closeness to God or intimacy with God is immediately suspect. This wariness and awe shape the way in which blessings are recognized, expressed and bestowed on others. A blessing is a means of acknowledging what God is doing or what God has done. 'Blessed be the LORD, for he has heard the sound of my pleadings,' says the Psalmist (Psalm 28.6). Or again, 'Blessed be the LORD, for he has wondrously shown his steadfast love to me when I was beset as a city under siege' (Psalm 31.21). A blessing may be pronounced by anyone, and may be bestowed on just about anyone or anything, including God, but the very act of blessing implies an acknowledgement that God, the fount of all blessing, is or has been or will be present in the situation, pouring out life and mercy, grace and peace.

Whatever prompts someone to pronounce a blessing, the occasion or event or action or gift is seen as God's work. The emphasis is on God's sovereignty, intention and initiative. The blessing describes what God has done (which is now being acknowledged), what God has given (for which thanks are now being offered), or what God has commanded to be done (and which is now being fulfilled). This is important: however it is phrased, the blessing assumes that the power and benefit are not in us, nor in what we hold, but in God and God alone.

Blessings occur in many stories, sometimes at the 'turning point' of the tale, as when Abraham's servant meets Rebekah (Genesis 24.26–27), or when David meets Abigail (1 Samuel 25.32–34), where the blessing is a reminder that God is present at the 'turning points' – the 'kairos moments' – of our own story, when a choice must be made, a new direction can be taken, if a transformation is to occur. And sometimes there is a blessing at the end of the story, when an alliance, a marriage, or the birth of a child suggests the opening of a new, God-given future (e.g. Exodus 18.10–11; Ruth 4.14–15; 1 Samuel 25.39). The blessing marks the moment, drawing attention to what it reveals about God's nature, actions and purposes. In that sense, it is a way of hallowing time: of declaring that God is Lord of the whole human story – acting in events, effecting change, bearing our concerns, turning the world upside down. A blessing thanks God for giving us life and governing proceedings in order to bring us to this moment and all it contains.

It is possible that Jesus' prayer was a 'blessing' of this kind. To us, the formal language and formulaic structure may seem too impersonal and objective to be truly heartfelt, but for the Jew, this 'distancing' is deliberate. It is a reminder that here we glimpse the divine, the holy, the transcendent and the eternal. Here in this moment, we encounter God who is wholly awesome, utterly Other.

Blessings acknowledge moments like my experience on the Athabasca Glacier: times when we are filled with awe by simply being alive and being where we are. To say that we are 'grateful' doesn't begin to express it. It is the recognition that by God's grace, we have been brought to this moment, we have glimpsed God's movements in the world, and we have received God's gifts. But the experience does not allow us to get comfortable. For with the sense of being connected to the Source of life, with its hints of closure and coming home, there is an even greater awareness that something new is beginning. Whether or not we take off our shoes, we know we are on holy ground.

Question: Do I have a sense of 'holy awe' at all that God has done and given to bring me to this moment? Have I ever had such an awareness? How does such an idea affect me? What does it change?

Reflection: Genesis 24.1–27. Abraham's servant rejoices that God has led him to his goal.

May my heart kneel in wonder to know you, O God;
Source of all blessing; river of my delight.
You are the sea of gladness in which I swim;
a fountain in which I can play.

May my mind find its centre in your peace, O God;
Feast of all fruitfulness; banquet of bread and wine.
You are the spread of plenty that will nourish and feed;
a table at which I am satisfied.

May my soul steer its course by your radiance, O God;
Light of our night road; guide to our right course.
You are the sign which calls us out, calls us on;
the lamp by the door which is home.

The truth of God and the truth of ourselves

On two other, similar, occasions, Mark uses another word: '*eucharisteo*' ('giving thanks') for the way Jesus prays. In the feeding of the four thousand, Jesus 'gives thanks' for the loaves (8.6); and at the Last Supper, he 'gives thanks' over the cup (14.23). In fact, Mark appears to regard '*eulogeo*' and '*eucharisteo*' as interchangeable terms. Both belong to a group of words, all beginning with the prefix *eu*, which circle around the idea of that which is done well, which is beneficial, beautiful, desirable, delightful, generous and benevolent. Such words encourage us to imagine Jesus' praying as words of grace expressing a spirit of profound gratitude for all the gifts of God. And, of course, it is from '*eucharisteo*' that we derive the term 'eucharist' for the sacrament of Holy Communion. So it is worth pausing to consider how Jesus might have 'given thanks' as he faced the multitude with the bread in his hand.

The Hebrew words for 'thanks' or 'thanksgiving' are rooted in the idea of admission or acknowledgement: that is, the admission that we have received and benefited from what has been given to us, so that we wish to express our appreciation, or our unworthiness to receive such generosity. This admission is vital because it turns us toward the one – or One – we want to thank and shows them that we are ready to receive. We are thankful, or penitent and thankful, and we are willing to acknowledge the truth about who we are and how we are.

This is where prayer begins. Truth is 'good soil' in which a relationship can grow. From this basis, a life-giving process can develop. But, to be accurate, there are several forms of truth which are relevant and which we must be ready to acknowledge. There is the truth of ourselves, our situation and what we hold in our hands. There is the truth of any others who may be involved or concerned. And there is the truth of God. All these various truths are related, but they are not the same. Our task in prayer is to hold them together, with honesty, discernment and trust.

We can see this pattern in the Book of Psalms: the admission that on the one hand, 'this is who God is', and on the other hand that 'this is who I am' or 'this is where we are'. Some psalms see the 'truth of God' in adoration, thanksgiving and praise. Others see 'the truth of ourselves' with a searing – even savage – honesty. But the 'truth of God' is not always seen in positive terms; and the 'truth of ourselves' is not always negative. Sometimes the truth is that God is hidden, silent or indifferent, and we deserve a better deal than the one we are getting. The psalms acknowledge all these various 'truths', laying them down side by side in a manner which can create abrupt shifts in tone and content within the space of a few lines. (See, for example, Psalms 22 or 36.)

Reading them, we can find this combination of radical honesty and different truths puzzling or even disturbing. The 'truth' of one moment may not be the 'truth' of the next. The 'truth' for one person may not be the 'truth' for all. There may be 'truth' that we are not yet willing to acknowledge. And gradually we realize that what the psalms are teaching us is that all the various forms of truth we experience must be acknowledged, even when we do not see how they are connected, let alone how the contradictions between them can be resolved.

The more we read the psalms with the intention of praying them, the more we realize that prayer is a journey into a deeper understanding of truth. Progress is made not by removing obstacles or resolving contradictions, but by admitting the truth of each moment, each person, each encounter, each word of the Lord, even when these truths conflict with one another. Not surprisingly, this approach is consistent with the stories in the Hebrew scriptures, where all the characters, including God and the servants of God, are presented with the same radical honesty. Various voices and points of view are set down side by side even when they do not agree.

Yet these stories (such as those which cluster around Abraham, Jacob, Moses, Samuel, David, Solomon, Elijah and Elisha) also show us how people can be brought to the point where they are willing to acknowledge another form of 'truth' alongside their own, and that when they do, something happens as a result of the encounter: something that is fresh and new. The stories show us how the process works, and how wonderfully it can work. Where two truths collide and interact with one another, the way in which we handle that encounter can enable a connection to be formed, and from that connection, a new relationship can grow. A new direction can be chosen. New companionships can be established, new ways of working together emerge.

In particular, our willingness to acknowledge and hold together the 'truth of God' and 'the truth of ourselves' creates a connection which is life-giving for us and for others. Our willingness to hold these different truths together – in ourselves, in this moment – permits the life and love of God to reach us, touch us and change us; transforming our situation and even altering the course of our lives.

So it may be that when Mark speaks of Jesus 'giving thanks', he is drawing on this tradition, and wants us to see Jesus' prayer in these terms. Perhaps, as Jesus looks up to heaven, he acknowledges the two 'truths' that he sees in the situation.

Firstly, as the faithful Son, he sees the vast treasury of God's life, grace and compassion; brought to hand in the bountiful kingdom; a feast of good things where all will be welcomed and every need will be met. It is possible that he describes this vision in words of wonder, love, thankfulness, and praise, but we cannot be certain, because in the Hebrew tradition, people could be utterly honest with God. When they felt aggrieved, they said so. When life was not fair, they held God to account.

Secondly, as the faithful shepherd of the flock, Jesus sees their numbers and the depth of their need; their isolation in an uninhabited area; the nature and scale of the resources available to them. We can be reasonably certain that Jesus laid this before the Father, but we should not assume that he spoke of the crowd as inadequate or apathetic, as weak or guilty, as sinful or lost.

If his prayer was consistent with the tradition that formed him, its life-giving element would be truth: the 'truth of God' and the truth of the human situation, both acknowledged in full and laid out side by side, for all to see and make their own response. In doing this, he created the spiritual conditions for a miracle.

Question: What words might I use to describe the 'truth of God'? What words might I use to describe the 'truth of myself'? What is God doing, here and now, to meet me? What am I doing to put myself where God can meet me?

Reflection: Genesis 18.23–33. Abraham argues that God must be true to the divine nature. God must be God, just and merciful in the face of Sodom's wickedness.

What must God do to reach me
where I am?
Nothing, for God is already here,
around me, within me,
closer than the air I breathe,

the blood feeding my brain,
the nerves threaded beneath my flesh.
I cannot move apart from you, Lord,
for you are already ahead of me:
disclosing my thoughts to my stirring mind,
interpreting the world into forms that make sense;
my ally, my Advocate, my other, better Self,
living within my skin.

What must I do to allow God to reach me?
Only wake up, tune in,
answer the invitation,
turn up to the dance;
become aware of the partner
at my shoulder,
respond to the hand taking mine.

Always and everywhere

However we imagine Jesus praying as he takes the bread, Mark suggests that the prayer sprang from gratitude and praise. But how can he stand in that place, with so much need before him, and so little in his hands with which to meet it, and *thank* God?

Even if Jesus frankly acknowledges insecurity and doubt, calls God to account for allowing the situation to develop, recalls the promises of scripture and proclaims what only God can do, some would still question his integrity. For at best, the five loaves and two fish can only symbolize his vision of God's feast, the possibility of a big feed, his longing for it, his commitment to making it real. They are not, in themselves, a feast for the multitude. Indeed, from another point of view, they could be seen as representing the need of the crowd, their raw unsatisfied yearning, their hunger. That being so, how can he thank God for so little?

When I became a member of the Methodist Church in 1977, the form of Holy Communion used in the church I attended was the liturgy contained in the then recently published *Methodist Service Book*.[1] As I was new to Methodism, I accepted this liturgy as a 'given'. Because I was also new to the whole idea of Holy Communion, this liturgy formed my understanding of the sacrament. And one particular phrase, from the beginning of the 'great prayer of thanksgiving', became seared into my consciousness. 'Always and everywhere': the idea that always and everywhere we could – should – offer

God thanks and praise. Always? Everywhere?

A few years later, I attended a residential conference for young adults led by the Revd Sister Mary Holliday. She had suggested that we bring photographic slides and taped music to entertain ourselves on the Saturday evening. We showed the slides and played the music in a random sequence, deriving much interest, and some amusement, from the juxtapositions that resulted. That is, until the moment when the image on the screen was a picture of Aberfan, showing the slagheap that had buried the village school, and the music that was playing was the 'Hallelujah Chorus' from Handel's *Messiah*.

The combination caused a most profound disquiet. At the end of the showing, Mary encouraged us to talk through our feelings. There was a long, wandering, inconclusive discussion which began and ended at much the same place: that our first thought had been that that we could not possibly hold together the 'Hallelujah Chorus' and the picture of Aberfan; and that our second thought had been that somehow, we had to do so, or, perhaps more accurately, that we had to try. It was not easy – we did not see how – and in many ways it felt offensive even to make the attempt; and yet we could not avoid the endeavour. For both the 'hallelujah' and the intolerable tragedy are truth. Both are part of human experience. If we want to be 'true' to the whole of what it means to be human, let alone be true to our faith in God, we have to respect both extremes and in some fashion do justice to both.

The very existence of these two extremes of human experience is deeply troubling. It is as though the highs and lows of life are filed in separate boxes and we become very uncomfortable whenever we are required to hold and consider them side by side, or relate them to one another in any way at all. This divide affects us at every turn: physically, emotionally, intellectually, morally, socially, spiritually. While we struggle to comprehend ideas which are so utterly opposed, our conflicting emotions tear us apart, robbing us of peace, leaving us anxious and insecure.

Rather than live in such chaos, we tend to restrict our vision to one part of the total spectrum. We diminish or deny the extremes which make us uneasy. We distance ourselves from experiences not our own. We put 'holy' things into their own separate compartment. We tend to focus on one 'truth' or one 'reality' at a time. We prefer the safe, the comfortable, the familiar.

We do this to survive, but the strategy has its price. Our experience covers a vast spectrum, from the absolutely mysterious to the utterly mundane. If we focus on one part of the spectrum, we neglect others, and we tend to lose sight of the spectrum as a whole. If we experience a great deal of one extreme, we may end up denying that the other exists at all. When we are enjoying ourselves, we can be so caught up in our joy that we not only forget our own suffering but lose the ability to empathize with the suffering of others. On the other hand, when we are miserable, we can feel as if we have lost the art of ever being happy again; and we can feel as though no one else has the right to be happy either.

T.S. Eliot observed that human beings 'cannot bear very much reality'.[2] He was right. But that is the essence of the spiritual task, to 'bear' the whole of reality as God gives it, and as we see it, feel it, live it, remember it, long for it. We 'bear' reality as others experience it, too, and as we experience it together.

It is a task which requires spiritual courage: to resist the narrowing of our vision; to receive the Other; to enter into a story that is not our own. In order to fulfil this task, we must explore and express both the heights and depths of human experience – and everything between – and do so when the very words we would use fail us; when the challenge is overwhelming and the questions are unanswerable.

How can we do this? Why should we bother? What is the point of exposing ourselves to joy or pain that is not our own? How can we bear so much upheaval? And how dare we be honest before God if what we want to express is anger, anguish or agony?

Questions like this become the main substance of our praying, since the more we learn about the world, the more we absorb not only its riches but its atrocities, too. We can get to the point where such knowledge is unbearable. How can we hold such wealth and, at the same time, such suffering? How can we relate the two extremes? Seeing what human beings are capable of doing to one another, how can we see such things, acknowledge the truth of such things, feel such things, bear such things – and in the next breath, praise?

Reflection: Ezra 3.10–13. As the foundation of the new temple is laid, the peoples' rejoicing is mixed with their grief.

> Prayer, like a line shot from earth to heaven,
> or a ladder dropped from heaven to earth,
> connects the two extremes of our awareness.
>
> The summits to which we aspire,
> the Everests of beauty, holiness, peace;
> ideas and acts which represent all that is good,
> all that we dream of becoming, or building;
> all that we mean by God; all that God has shown us;
> our encounter with the divine, the holy,
> the transcendent, the eternal;

the One who is All and wholly awesome,
utterly Other.

And the desolate abyssal plain
of our intensive and intended cruelty;
the potential laid waste by bitterness;
those who have taken pleasure in destroying innocence
and in plundering a treasure not their own;
those who have invaded homes and hopes,
distorting minds and butchering bodies;
those whose vision has divided partnerships,
isolated resistance, annihilated trust
and made a virtue of organized wrong;
empires which have ground humanity
to the bone, and allowed the dust and ash
to blow away.

Prayer, like a line shot from earth to heaven,
or a ladder dropped from heaven to earth,
connects the two extremes of our existence.

Contradiction unresolved

Offering any kind of thanksgiving for the bread lays bare the extremes of our experience. Good and evil. Riches and poverty. Health and sickness. Justice and oppression. Life and death. On the one hand, our awareness of all that is life-giving, prosperous and peaceful. On the other, the fact that resources are distributed unequally, unfairly and that so often there is not enough to go around.

Extremes do not meet easily. It can be like stumbling over a starving child on your way to a five-course dinner, or discovering a drunk sleeping rough on the church steps on Christmas morning, or watching your vegetable garden shrivel during a hose-pipe ban while your neighbour fills his swimming pool and waters his lawn. When contradictions meet, they clash and collide, stirring up envy, anger, protest, guilt and grief. They arouse tension and conflict within us, and between ourselves and those around us. In our better moments, such passions spur us into asking the essential questions about how we can bear one another's burdens and share resources so that we live together in prosperity and peace. But we do not always live up to our highest ideals, and in the hurly-burly of everyday life we do not always know how to handle this unwelcome turbulence. We may not even recognize what is

106

going on or what it is doing to us. We cannot always prevent our reactions deteriorating into violence.

Yet Jesus brings these two extremes together and holds them together, in an act of prayer. He does it as one stage in the process of applying faith to his situation. It is a decisive step in a new direction which will eventually lead both shepherd and flock into an altered 'landscape'. But it also raises the stakes.

We know that the story ends with everyone being fed. But the crowd doesn't know that and neither do the disciples. And if Jesus is fully human, then he doesn't know that for certain either. So to many of those present, Jesus' action would appear illogical and unrealistic. Accepting the truth of the situation might make some sort of sense, but giving thanks for it – any of it – does not.

Generally speaking, we do not find it too hard to give thanks when resources are plentiful and our hunger is satisfied. It is far harder to give thanks when resources are scarce, we have not been given our share, and we are not convinced that the limited amount available will be distributed fairly. Giving thanks in such circumstances tends to imply that we are grateful for everything the moment contains, whatever that might be and however it affects ourselves or others. It can seem as though we are glossing over the presence of injustice, hunger or grief; as though we are condoning situations and behaviours which cannot or should not be condoned. Such a denial is a smack in the face if we are suffering. If someone fails to assert our rights, they also fail to affirm our value as human beings, diminishing us further.

However much the truth of God may inspire or require our adoration, where the truth of the human condition is filled with pain we must consider how we hold these two truths – or versions of the same truth – together. It is necessary to do justice to both: in expressing gratitude to God, to acknowledge the suffering; and in offering petitions for those who suffer, to pray with hope. But giving thanks sharpens the contrast between the plenty which God commands and the dearth we are experiencing. To pronounce a blessing can be seen as simplistic, naive, deceitful, deluded or denial; a degree of acceptance which others find awkward, troubling, provocative or offensive. However careful our words, we may assume a gratitude beyond what others can offer.

Harder still are those situations where thanksgiving would be so inappropriate, insensitive or inflammatory that it is impossible to offer it at all. Because we have efficient global communication networks, we are no longer innocent: we have seen how defenceless we are against natural phenomena such as hurricanes and tsunami. Worse, we have seen how human beings willingly embrace the dynamics of death, perpetrating malice, cruelty and abuse; instigating atrocities; organizing genocide.

Evasion is no longer possible, and in the face of such suffering, thanksgiving of any kind – however sensitive – can seem misplaced. Anger and anguish can bleach all good from the world to the point where we feel that goodness can no longer exist: that light, benevolence, love or beauty no longer have any *right* to exist; that to look for anything life-giving is evading the truth of death. Instead, we feel that our response should be shaped by silence, humility and self-restraint.

In such a context, thanksgiving becomes a task that is complex, subtle, nuanced, and easily misunderstood. We cannot simply claim that 'life goes on' and give thanks regardless. Such an attitude not only denies the intensity of human suffering: it also denies the compassion of God as we have seen it in Christ. There is no way around the paradox: celebration sharpens the conflict between the 'hallelujah' and the holocaust. Either we praise a God who has little interest in our suffering, whose judgement overrules any compassion, who has chosen not to intervene or who is powerless to do so; or the scale of human suffering and guilt is proof that a loving God does not, cannot, exist to be praised.

The contradiction remains unresolved. There is no easy, straightforward way to offer God's feast to those who have been starved, or who, for whatever reason, are starving themselves. If we advocate abundance, then some will take offence. It is not always possible to avoid this, but it is essential that we try, that we strive to avoid causing *unnecessary* offence.

This means respecting the sensitivities of others and the possibility that they might not react to a situation as we do. If we invite them to share the heights of our hope, we must acknowledge the depths of their suffering. We must do justice to their truth as well as our own, even though we feel the contradiction between them. We must not rush to close this contradiction so that we feel more comfortable. The gulf between the love of God and the grim struggle of so many lives is part of the truth to which we must be faithful. We do not honour God by celebrating in any way which diminishes, dismisses or denies it.

If we persist in prayer, this fissure between the grace of God and the pain of the world will rip us apart. If we wish to be faithful, we must let it do so, even though we will experience its effects at every level of our being. We do not seek dislocation and discomfort for their own sake, but we accept them because doing so is the only way in which we can remain loyal to the truth: the truth of God and the truth of the human condition. We live with the effects of this contradiction in every part of ourselves, making it our offering, in the hope that as we do so, God who is love is somehow fashioning a holistic and ultimately satisfactory response – though, to be frank, we cannot yet see it. And perhaps we never will.

Nevertheless, we trust. We trust God, who asks this service of us as our loving response to the suffering of others. We trust Jesus, who shows us that the contradiction between the life-giving abundant love of God and the life-draining suffering of humanity requires the offering of our whole selves. As we experience this chasm in the whole of our being, so our response becomes holistic too, for we cannot bridge that gulf with reason nor is it adequate to fill it with feeling.

Persisting with this degree of honesty is difficult. We are tempted (and I use that word deliberately) to resolve the contradiction by limiting the reality, scale or impact of one extreme or the other. At one end of the spectrum, we persuade ourselves that the gospel of abundance does not apply to us, here and now. We say that miracles don't happen. We teach people not to hope too much. We discourage them from dreaming dreams. We tell them that they must be realistic. We counsel them to accept their limitations. At the other end of the spectrum, we do not allow sufficient time and space to express, explore and address the wounds of the world. In our prayers and in our pastoral work we leap too swiftly from Palm Sunday (or Maundy Thursday) to Easter Day, forgetting the long night journey which happened between, and thereby abandon those who are taking the slow path through that labyrinth.

However, by moderating these extremes to make ourselves more comfortable, and by diminishing or denying the truth that the contradiction between them remains unresolved, we limit God's ability to give us life. On the one hand, the abundance of God is the *life* of God. This is what we have to offer: if we do not have this, we have nothing. On the other hand, it is in steadfastly paying attention to the places of dearth, and to the people who are dying there, that we learn how to serve the God of abundance, and all that God can do. We learn this from those who are suffering there, if we are willing to respect their dignity and listen to their wisdom. And we learn it from our anguished powerlessness; from the effort it takes to stop, to be still, to let go of our impatience so that we can pay attention.

No, the value of Jesus' life, teaching, ministry, mission and Passion lies precisely in the way in which he honoured the extremes of his experience, and the truth that they remained unresolved. By holding them together in himself, he created a connection between them, and by paying steady attention to each he showed us how to do justice to both; how to hold them together in a way which releases the love of God to bring life to the point of need.

Question: How do I pay attention to the two 'poles' of my experience and to the contradiction between them? What does it cost? Are there ways in which I could protect myself less and trust God more?

Reflection: Psalm 137. Praise, grief and the longing for vengeance.

The value of Jesus' life,
teaching, ministry and Passion
lies in the way he honoured
the heights of heaven
and the depths of our human hells,
and by holding them together,
in himself,
became the bridge.

He showed us that it is by
paying a steady attention to each,
and allowing the gulf between
to tear us apart,
that we do justice to both,
and allow the love of God
to reach the point
of death,
still bearing
the light
of life.

Learning to see

The contradiction between our experience on the one hand of wonder, grace and God, and – on the other – of loss, grief, suffering and death is not resolved in a manner which answers all our questions; nor in a fashion which proves, beyond all reasonable doubt, that God loves us and gives us good things. The gap between joy and sorrow is never completely closed in this life – not for everyone, or for all to see.

Even the grace of God has not achieved this, for in order to watch the Spirit at work, we must be willing to see. Even the cross of Christ has not bridged this gulf, for the Christian claim that the Passion of Jesus has dealt with evil, sin and death once and for all, remains a statement of faith. As such, it has enormous transformative power, but that does not make it a fact that everyone must acknowledge whether they like it or not.

So the contradiction remains, despite all our efforts to get our heads, or our hearts, around it. Humanists still debunk God, philosophers still debate the problem of evil, and theologians still write books attempting to explain why good people suffer and why prayers are not always answered in the way we want them to be. And so they should. For the most part, these are honest attempts to honour the whole truth of human experience.

Inevitably, we get entangled in the same endeavour, because joy and sorrow are the extremes of our personal experience, too. Adoration and desolation are related to one another because we –you and I – experience them both. The highway to Zion and the road through the valley of misery run through the same human hearts. At times the contradiction is overwhelming. We can feel ripped to shreds by divergent points of view, turbulent emotions, the sheer variety of opinions, attitudes, words and deeds. We are not leaves drifting powerlessly on a stream, however, but travellers pushing through a storm. Even as we are battered by gusts of wind and rain, I am myself; you are who you are. It is by paying attention to this essential truth of ourselves that we become more consistent, coherent and centred.

The challenge is to be fully alive. As Michel Quoist wrote in his seminal collection of prayers in the 1960s, 'Don't sleep any more'.[3] We choose to be alert, awake, aware. Each moment has its thought, its mood, its task. This moment, joy; the next, sorrow. We are invited to enter fully and honestly into each – whatever it brings – with all our capacities and powers. To receive what life puts in our hands. To 'admit' it, admit the truth of it and, wherever possible, admit the blessing of it. To acknowledge it, celebrate it and give thanks for it, even when we do so through gritted teeth, or through a tissue of tears.

In this moment, be aware of one thing. Pay attention to one thing. One person. One happening. One situation. One response. One task. Sit light to the past and the future. It is in the present moment that we live. Here and now, we bless God for giving us life and bringing us to this moment with all that we hold in our hands.

Offering this obedience – this way of looking and listening, the attention of a disciple to the presence of the Master – we can be surprised to discover that what we hold can indeed absorb our full awareness The moment is larger than it appears. It contains more than we recognized. It is richer than we thought. Paying attention feeds us.

As a child growing up in the nineteenth century, John Ruskin was allowed very few toys. So from a very early age, he passed the time examining the patterns he found in bed covers, clothes and wallpapers; tracing the squares and comparing the colours of a carpet, exploring the knots in the wood of the floor, or counting the bricks in the house across the road. He learned to notice such things, to appreciate the wealth that there is in detail. By paying attention, he learned to see the world: really see it. Ordinary events watched from his window, such as the filling of a water-cart, became the cause of fascination and excitement.

As a result, when something more unusual came along, he saw things that others did not see. When he was three and a half years old, he was taken to visit an artist, Mr Northcote, to have his portrait painted. Instead of being overawed by the formality of the occasion, or bored by having to sit still for a long period, as any normal child might be, John studied the carpet on the floor, and then asked the artist why there were holes in it. What began as a way of passing the time became a way of seeing the world which allowed Ruskin, as he grew up, to champion new ways of addressing the social and spiritual challenges of his age. Paying attention taught him to see, and seeing made him an artist and social reformer.

Of course, deprivation is not a good thing in itself. But that is just the point. What we 'hold' in this moment will not necessarily be good, or good enough. Certainly, it is unlikely to be perfect. So often, we assume that this lack of perfection is the reason we cannot achieve what we want to achieve. But is it really? What if it is our fear, and the way fear makes us feel – angry, irritated, impatient, bored – which makes it hard for us to work creatively with what comes to us? What if our task is to identify our fears and let go of them; to get beyond them so that we can work with the moment until it expresses God's vision of how the world should be?

The art of abundance is in paying attention. Quality of life, richness of experience and excellence of achievement do not arise from our attempts to control circumstances and events, but from the depth of our attention to what is passing before our eyes and through our hands. We begin by paying attention to what we already 'hold in our hands', and by paying attention to it all. This is what God has already given to fill us. As we 'unpack' it, 'chew it over' and 'digest it', we are fed.

We can use odd moments to practise – we do not have hours; the hours are spent doing other things. The moments add up, though, and using them teaches us how to use the hours when they do become available. Paying attention to the moment, we receive life like a child. We look at the world as if for the first time. Everything is fresh and fascinating; everywhere around there are marvels. The gift is not just what is in the box, but the box itself and the paper it is wrapped in, too. We set aside the ways of seeing we have inherited from others and re-open the eye of wonder.

As we do so, we explore our own way of seeing, and then, in expressing it, release our own artistry. An artist is anyone who is learning to see. Those who pay attention to what they are seeing and how they are looking, however, can disclose the secrets of the universe, the secrets of life itself. We become more creative as our attention deepens. The eye of the Creator is the eye of a child. Children lead the wise.

Question: What are the feelings which make it hard for me to pay attention to what is before me? What are the feelings which make it hard for me to 'receive' what is given, and work with it creatively? What do I think might happen if I let these feelings go? Are they pointing me to areas where I need to increase my trust?

Reflection: Genesis 28.10–17. The place of stones becomes the gate of heaven.

> God is love.
> So what?
>
> Unless God loves me
> enough to meet my needs,
> why should I bother?
> Unless God gives good things,
> not just to people in general,
> everyone else, those in the past
> or those who are special,
> but to me, where I am,
> right now,
> tired and hungry:
> why should I care?
> Unless I see the links in the chain
> which lets the love of God reach out
> to me, for me,
> why should I be glad?
>
> Following your lead,
> I place my trust
> in a pair of untried, untested wings,
> acting as if
> they will bear my weight,
> the strain of all I hold,
> my burden
> of incoherent prayer.

Seeing abundance

The first responsibility of the spiritual life is a commitment to honesty: above all, honesty before God, which is only possible if we are honest with ourselves. This means becoming alert to the present moment and aware of what it contains. It means paying attention to our highest aspirations and our most terrible fears; to the very best and the very worst of our experience and everything in between. We pay attention so that we see the moment clearly and accurately, so that we remain alert, though this is hard as well as rewarding. We let go of our illusions to face the truth of God; and let go of our pretensions so that we can face the truth of ourselves.

Our commitment to honesty means that we accept the gulf between the wonder which inspires our longing and what we actually have in our hands. We do not deny this chasm, nor attempt to diminish it. We do not evade the truth that this gulf divides nations, churches and our own hearts; nor that it echoes with anguish and seethes with violence. We do not attempt to hide this truth, nor hide from it. We deal with what is. When we look to God, we see the feast: when we look to the world, we see the hungry multitude: when we look in our hands, we see five loaves and two fish.

We choose to see things as they are so that we can pay attention to them in a manner which is life-giving: examining, expressing, exploring it all; rejoicing in all that is good, choosing to see potential in the most unlikely situations; acting as if that potential is real. We invest in life wherever we find it. We 'bear' reality as a woman bears a child: providing it with a warm, safe space in which to grow; carrying it through a period of gestation; nourishing it from ourselves; relating to it; growing with it, bringing it forth, letting it go. Mundane details become the raw material with which we work. We collaborate with the Spirit to create an abundance which contains the life of God. We 'bear' reality, and the way in which we bear it can enable God to transform it.

The transfiguring encounter does not happen automatically, however. Like the people of Israel as they prepared to enter the Promised Land, we have to 'choose life' repeatedly (Deuteronomy 30.15–20) if we wish to enjoy the benefits God makes available to us. We remain aware that we have other choices, that we are not required to see this moment, this person, this situation as full of possibility – like a seed – but that we choose to do so because this is how we remain faithful to the vision of God, to the teaching and example of Jesus, and to the way that the Holy Spirit is prompting us to respond.

This is what sets Jesus apart: the quality of attention he offers to the moment and all it contains. He respects all the various truths he encounters: the truth of God, the truth of the hungry crowd, the truth of the situation, and his own truth, too. He respects the powers of life and death. He allows it all to inform his response. But he chooses, as the basis of that response, to act as if life is present, even if the evidence suggests that life is just about extinct. He chooses to sow life, sustain life, develop life, magnify life; acting as if it is God's purpose to nourish life indiscriminately, regardless of whether or not it acknowledges the divine. He acts as if life is always capable of becoming abundant, even where that seems unlikely. He chooses to act as if the abundant love of God will ensure that the abundant life of God is always available, accessible and attainable. He acts as if the grace of God will always have the final word.

Consider Jesus' response to the disciples. He may have been irritated or disheartened by their attitude, but, if so, he handles his emotions and gets beyond them. He chooses to see these men as God sees them, as abundant rather than impoverished, as people of potential, who are growing, changing, on the move and capable of learning from their mistakes. And then he acts as if that vision is true, so that they begin to see it, too. He demonstrates faith in them. He challenges but does not criticize, encouraging them to confront their anxieties and replace them with trust. He models for them an alternative way of seeing their situation and, rather than excluding them, he gives them a role consistent with their calling, their training and their previous experience. But they are tired, so he does not overload them with responsibility. Instead, he gives them things they can do. He instructs them to find out what resources are available. He tells them to get everyone to sit down. He gives them the loaves to set before the people. He involves them in the process which makes the miracle happen. He shows them that even there, they have alternatives. They can choose abundance. They can celebrate God's vision of abundant life. That vision can be realized, even in the face of the multitude.

Consider Jesus' attitude to the crowd. He recognizes that they need a specialized form of help – the leadership of a shepherd – but he does not see them as limited by any of their other needs. There may be weakness, disease, poverty, corruption and sin amongst them, but these things do not define their condition or determine their potential. Instead, he chooses to see them as God sees them, as people made in the divine image, heirs to abundant life, and God's partners in creation. They are hungry for life in all its fullness; inspired by the vision of the feast; eager to know how they can amend their lives and improve their circumstances. He teaches them many things because he sees them as capable of learning them.

For Jesus, the 'facts' are only part of the truth of the situation. He chooses to base his response on the most positive truth he can see. He chooses to see abundance, even though the resources given are less than the need. He chooses to receive them and accept them, even though they are not enough to improve the situation. He chooses to give thanks, even though he does not have enough in his hands to bring about the necessary change. Yet he does this, not because he is a fool or a charlatan, but because he believes in the purposes and promises of God.

Such an attitude is only possible as a process of faith: a life of faith: made up of many acts of faith, one step after another. Jesus takes the bread into his hands because, despite its many deficiencies, he sees what he is holding as a gift. This acceptance is not simplistic, but complex. He is not being naive or dishonest. He is not denying the size or scale of the crowd's hunger, nor the fact that the available resources are inadequate. Rather, he acknowledges the various truths of the situation, but then chooses to see, think and act as if he possesses plenty. He anticipates the feast. He blesses God as the One who is the Source of life and Lord of all, and who has brought them to that moment. He gives thanks for the bread as the bounty God has given to begin the process of feeding the crowd.

If Jesus had been asked whether his cup was half empty or half full, he would see the abundance. Every time.

Question: Do I see myself as 'abundant', as 'larger' than my fear, as life-giving? Do I find it easy to think that God sees me like this? If not, why not?

Reflection: Psalm 23. The shepherd leads us so that we are renewed.

> Seeing myself as you see me,
> heir to the wealth of Eternity,
> sustained by the Infinite,
> always and endlessly Beloved:
> I can do this thing before me,
> I can give myself,
> I can give my whole self
> to this.
>
> Seeing myself as you see me,
> immersed in the richest environment,
> informed by all I have learned,
> enlightened by all I have absorbed:
> I can do this thing before me,
> I can give myself,
> I can give my whole strength
> to this.
>
> Seeing myself as you see me,
> nourished by so many foods,
> enlivened by such lavish loving,
> sated with the bread that satisfies:
> I absorb as much as I can hold,
> I am filled up, fulfilled,
> content.

Seeing myself as you see me,
abundance is no longer a dream
out there, behind the horizon;
beyond me, promised
but not yet known.
It has become my experience,
as I do this thing before me,
as I give myself,
as I give my whole life
to this.

Chapter 6
The Way of Jesus

It was the way he did things. What he did, but also the way he did it. Not just the fact that he listened, but the way he listened, as if he was receiving what you had to say, drawing it in and accepting it because it was true for you and therefore it mattered to him – whether or not he liked it. He wasn't there to tell us what he liked or disliked, whether or not he approved. The point was he listened as if it mattered, as if we mattered.

He listened, he spoke, he acted the same way. He accepted things. He accepted whatever he found – in a situation or a person – and until it was proved otherwise, he saw it as all good. A gift from God. A blessing. I never heard him moan or complain or grouse. He didn't bear grudges or hold on to a bad opinion about someone. He was always willing to see the best in them, and even if they abused him or resisted him or turned away, he did not take it personally. He saw the positive in everything and everyone, even when it was difficult. Even when it was an effort. Even when it cost him.

And yet, he wasn't stupid and he wasn't naive. He knew what people were capable of doing. He saw the pride in them. He knew how deep their malice ran. He knew people could be callous, cruel and cold; how a man could cut his wife with a word. It grieved him because he felt it was unnecessary and unjustified, but it never surprised him how vicious and violent people could become. He always stepped in, if he could, to disarm a situation with a quip or a joke. He never started a fight, and if he saw one developing, he would diffuse it before it could get going. Not that he was a coward. Far from it. It took courage to face down Simon when he was in a mood – he was a big man in every sense – or to distract the Sons of Thunder when they took offence and started growling.

He could get angry himself, but it was always at what had been dumped on someone else, never at what was dumped on him. He got angry when he saw how those who were already suffering were made to suffer more by the pettiness and prejudice of those around them. He was furious whenever he saw the sick being penalized, or those with leprosy being excluded, or those who had never had a chance in life being dismissed as sinners because of what they had to do to survive. He understood how people became prostitutes or beggars, collaborators or thieves. He knew what made them, and what they wanted, and because of that, he could talk to them, reach them, influence them.

He was always thankful. Grateful for anything anyone did for him, glad of any help. He was never slow to show his appreciation. He knew how to bestow a blessing. Children loved him, because he saw the world as they did, as a place full of marvel and miracle; lit up, as if from within, with a diffused wealth. He was always eager to examine, explore, investigate, inquire. There was always something new to wonder at. He took delight in the simplest things. He paid attention to everything. He noticed details.

He valued generosity in others because he knew what generosity can cost. He valued it, especially, in those who could least afford to give. He never underestimated a person's capacity for loving, for forgiving, for serving others. Yes, he knew people were capable of great wrong, but he also knew people could do the right thing, and he did everything he could to encourage it. He believed that we could live beyond our history, our constraints, our disabilities, our time. He believed anyone could.

But he never forced us. He loved us as we were. That was his greatest gift to us. He never demanded that we change. He loved us as we came to him: poor, maimed, fallible and frail. He made it clear that he loved us and would go on loving us whatever happened, whatever we did; if we stayed with him or if not, wherever we went. His commitment to us was unending: awesome in its height and depth and breadth and power; a glimpse of the love of God, vast beyond our imagining. And yet he was infinitely gentle with those who were tired, oppressed, ill or grieving; those who could not cope with anything more; those who could not face the thought of doing things differently, those who could not see how another life was possible at all. He understood what it was to feel overwhelmed.

And so he did not press us. Challenged us, yes, if he felt we could take it, but he never made us feel that, unless we changed, he would stop loving us. No, he wasn't like that. He loved us to the end. It was just that he did not want us to remain helpless and hopeless. He wanted us to know that the promises of God were available. That we could access them, claim them, enjoy them. He wanted us to have everything that was ours. All the blessings. All the promises. The Kingdom of God. Shalom. Wholeness, justice, abundance, health and peace.

But he knew we can only claim these things if we feel able to ask. If we are convinced that God wants us to have them. We can only claim them if we feel that God will welcome us, accept us, value us and honour us. And for that to happen, the indestructible and indefinable grace of God's love has to be made personal, practical, real. It has to be given a form that makes sense. That matters to me. Each one of us has to realize: 'This is for me. Even me. As I am. Even as I am, here and now.'

For some of us, learning to ask took a long time. Even learning that we could ask took all the time he was able to give. But he never pushed us further or faster than we were willing to go. He left us in charge of our own destiny.

After all, he hadn't called us to become an army or a campaign or an organization or an empire. He didn't call us to be anything other than ourselves. That was what we were with him: a company of people travelling the road of life, learning how to be ourselves; how to love God with the whole of ourselves; how to love our neighbour as ourselves. This was the great adventure to which he called us: the task of being the people God had made us to be. Neither more, nor less.

And this is what he taught us. Faith is not about what we have, but what we do with it. The way we use what we have: the way we receive it and give thanks for it, seeing it as a gift, an abundance, a treasure, enough; then applying it, working with it, investing it, keeping on keeping on. Faith is this way of loving ourselves, loving those around us, loving the world we live in. The Way of Jesus is faith from beginning to end.

The gesture of commitment

Having taken the bread into his hands and given thanks, Jesus' third action is to break the bread and give it to his disciples to distribute to the crowd. At the end of a long, hard working day, which has not turned out as he or his disciples expected, Jesus stands before five thousand tired, hungry people, with five loaves in his hands, and acts as if this tiny quantity of food is enough to feed them.

The sheer audacity of this action should give us pause. What on earth does he think he is doing? What do those around him think he is doing? What do any of them expect to happen?

Until this moment, he has kept his options open. Merely receiving the bread does not indicate what he intends to do with it. Nor does giving thanks. As soon as he takes action, however, he closes down every option but one. He constrains himself to a particular way of responding to the situation. He excludes all other possibilities.

The moment in which we take action is significant and scary, encompassing both magnificent potential, but also terrifying risk. We are making decisions which narrow down our options. We choose a door and go through it. What lies behind the doors we have not chosen? Would those possibilities have turned out better? We will never know.

In taking action, we accept the constraints of our situation, gather our courage, make a choice, and, for good or ill, plunge into the task of making something happen with what we have. We convert an insubstantial idea into something that is personal, practical, material. We turn something that is abstract, theoretical and imagined into flesh and blood, or paper and ink, or canvas and oil, or bricks and mortar, or some other specific form. To do this, we have to exclude other possible forms.

Some horses have to wear blinkers so that they run a straight race. Similarly, to take action, we have to edit our options and prioritize one. To act most effectively, we concentrate our powers to a single point: what we are doing in this moment, here and now. We do one thing at a time. If I am writing, I cannot be painting, even if part of me is longing to paint. If I am writing this book, I cannot be writing letters, even if there are people waiting to hear from me. If I am following this train of thought, I cannot be following another; and so on.

In taking action, we tune out the voice which says 'What if?' (What if I think about this some more? What if we wait a bit longer? What if another way is better? What if I make another choice altogether?) and we commit ourselves to *this* action in *this* moment with *these* materials. Once we have committed ourselves, we cannot turn back, not without loss. Very often, we cannot turn back at all. Whatever happens – however it turns out – the action we have chosen must take its course.

This is awesome because, however thorough our research, however careful our preparation and however detailed our planning, there is always a risk of failure. What we do may not work, or work as well as we hope. It may have consequences we have not foreseen, for others as well as ourselves. It may work well for a time, but then cease working. We may never know if it has worked or not. It may work very well indeed, but still not be enough for our purposes.

Taking action, we can no longer hide our plans, our intentions or our desires. Our view of the world comes out of our heads and is given shape in the world around us. Our inner world becomes – at least in part – our outer world; our values and vision emerge for all to see.

The upside is that the wealth inside us can be experienced by others, invested and enhanced, and used for our benefit and the common good. We can make something happen, achieve something worthwhile, make a difference to the lives of others, live our dream.

The downside is that our actions will be tested, evaluated and judged by other people, and because what we do is an expression of our vision and values – an intimate part of who we are – an evaluation of our performance can feel like a judgement on our worth as a person. It may even feel like an attempt to annihilate us.

The moment when we act, therefore, is significant and scary. It can feel as though the world is shifting on its axis, as though our survival hangs in the balance, as though life will never be the same again. This sounds daft, but it isn't. We are laying down our life as we have known it to take a new direction (8.34–38). We do not know what will happen. We cannot control the outcome, nor what it might cost us. Yet action is essential if truth is to be realized. It matters that we act.

It matters on the large scale: how dare we claim that God is love, joy, justice, truth, mercy, grace and peace, if we are not prepared to act on what we believe, to shape our lives and our relationships and the world around us according to that belief? If Jesus' vision of abundant life for all is ever to be realized, it must be earthed in the material world. Until we act, the gospel remains insubstantial: inspiring, perhaps, but no practical use to anyone; or, as one of my grandmothers used to say, 'too heavenly minded to be any earthly good'.

On a small scale, too, it matters that we act. Each of us is called to honour the truth of ourselves by becoming comfortable inside our own skin, occupying our personal space in the world, living a loving, creative life from the inside out (7.14–23). If our best thoughts and highest ideals are to achieve anything at all, they must be expressed in action. If our dream of what we might achieve or what God might be calling us to bring into being is to have any substance, we must act on it. I am the protagonist in my story, simply because it is my story, not yours. And your story is yours, not mine. The only person who can live your life is you. So live it!

Acting tests the vision, but, as we give our vision a specific shape, it feeds us; it is renewed and strengthened within us; it grows like a vigorous plant until it bears fruit (4.1–8, 14–20). Like a plant, if it is not growing, it is almost certainly dying. Unless our vision is revitalized by being earthed, regularly, in action, its power to inspire us and motivate us will drain away. In time it will become no more than a fantasy, and we will have lost, perhaps forever, the ability to transform ourselves and our circumstances; or, to put it another way: the ability to respond to God's infinite, transforming grace.

So it matters that we act; but it also matters *how* we act. We can misinterpret the compulsion to get on with it, to do something – anything – as long as we act. We can be tempted to act immediately, or to act in a way which we hope will produce swift results, simply because we are anxious, impatient or frustrated.

At a critical point in J.K. Rowling's 'Harry Potter' series, Harry's mentor, Professor Dumbledore, warns Harry and his friends that in the dark and difficult days ahead, they may face the choice between what is right and what is easy. Wise words. The critical ethical and moral choices we face are not necessarily between what is right and what is wrong. Rather, we must choose between what is average, mediocre, expected, the thing that 'everyone' does; and that other possibility which is more right, but also more difficult, because we have to think about it. We have to respond, rather than simply react; consider doing things differently. Alter a habit. Take responsibility for our action. Commit ourselves.

The temptation to react, or to act without thinking, is far stronger when we are under pressure, when we do not have – or dare not take – time to consider our response. Reacting is quick and efficient, which is why we have habits, routines and 'gut reactions' in the first place. But if we wish to live in the divine image, to be creative as God is creative, to follow the 'way' of Jesus, we need to consider how we react to particular contexts and particular people and ask whether there are times when we could take another road; a more uncertain, but ultimately more generous course; one that will lead us – and others – towards abundant life.

Question: Is there any context in which I know that action is required, but I am avoiding or putting off doing anything about it? What are the particular techniques I use to avoid taking action? Why do I use them?

Reflection: Exodus 3.7 – 4.17. Moses thinks of all sorts of reasons why he is not the right man for the job.

> I may not believe
> that I am lovely and beloved,
> but if I act as if I am loved,
> I can stop beating myself up
> for the mistakes I have made
> in the past.
> Start again from here.
> Make a new beginning.

> I may not believe
> that I am 'good enough' for this,
> but if I act as if I am,
> I can relax a little.
> Treat myself.
> Do something for the sheer fun of it.
> Laugh.
> Have a good time.

I may not believe
I have permission to do
what really matters to me,
but if I act as if I have,
investing time and money
in the things I enjoy –
hobbies, interests,
passions, relationships –
they give me life.

I may not believe
I have what it takes
to 'meet' the multitude,
but if I meet them,
we can take a step forward
together.

Taking another road

By breaking the bread and giving it to the disciples to distribute amongst the crowd, Jesus 'takes another road'. Indeed, some might argue that he has taken leave of his senses. Certainly, he has departed from the way that people normally think. How can he possibly expect that in dividing this small quantity of bread he will have enough to feed the crowd? The idea is improbable, irrational, absurd. Nevertheless, this is what he does. Why?

Well, what else could he have done? What were his other options – the ones he resisted or rejected?

He could have eaten the bread himself. We might consider this idea unthinkable, too shockingly selfish, but should we assume that the crowd or the disciples would have seen it that way? People can be astonishingly generous to those who reflect their values and vision, and often honour them with gifts of food, especially when a community gathers to eat together. There is little doubt that as 'shepherd' of the flock, Jesus represents their best hopes, their highest aspirations and their greatest desires. They have gone to considerable lengths to meet him, even following him out into a deserted place. Would they have objected if he had accepted the bread as a gift for his own use? Would they have considered it unfair or even out of the ordinary?

Perhaps not. But in any case, Jesus does the opposite. He demonstrates that, as the one who represents all that they honour and desire, he will not consume the best or largest share of the available resources himself, but rather ensure that these things are accessible to everyone. He shows them God's desire and purpose for them; God's vision of who they are and what they might become together.

As a second option, Jesus could have disposed of the bread in a ritual manner, to show the crowd that their gift was received and acknowledged by God and was reserved for God alone. Admittedly, it is not clear how he might have done this. In ancient times, he might have built an altar and burned the bread as an offering. But those days were past. The sacrificial system was now centralized in the Temple at Jerusalem, and Jesus was a teacher, not a priest. We cannot be certain what actions were available to him in this context, or what they would have conveyed.

Besides, by giving thanks, Jesus had already acknowledged that the bread was the gift of God. This blessing raises a question: why does God give us good things? So that they can be returned to God in sacrifice? So that they can be consumed by priests, religious leaders or those respected by the community? Jesus' action is his answer. He acts like David in the sanctuary of Nob, when he claimed the bread of the presence for himself and his tired, hungry men (1 Samuel 21.1–6, see Mark 2.23-28). He demonstrates that the resources God gives are not reserved for God, nor for religious officials or high-status individuals. They are to be made available to the people in their hour of need.

This leads to a third possibility, namely that Jesus could have sought out the frailest or most vulnerable individual in the crowd and given the food to them. This might have been welcomed, even applauded, as a prophetic sign of God's concern for the poorest of the poor, consistent with the Methodist dictum, 'Go not to those who need you, but to those who need you most.' But again, it is hard to see how this might have worked in practice, given that the crowd is already formed from people so keen to see Jesus that they followed him into the wild. Arguably he is already working where he is needed most, amongst the neediest of the needy. How can he discriminate further?

A fourth option is that he could have practised 'triage', dividing the crowd into three groups: a) those strong enough to manage without food, b) those so weak or sick that they would deteriorate whether or not they were fed, and c) borderline cases, where receiving food would make a significant difference to someone's survival.

Triage is a technique developed by battlefield surgeons, who have learned that some casualties can wait for treatment and some will die whatever is done for them; so medical staff concentrate on those patients for whom prompt attention will literally make the difference between life and death. However, triage requires a detached, objective assessment of people and their needs. It is a strategy used by carers whose resources are strictly limited. It may be pragmatic but it views individuals as cases, rather than as whole persons. In its most extreme form, it assumes that there is nothing to be gained from investing time and energy in those who are beyond saving.

Even if Jesus was familiar with this kind of thinking, it seems unlikely that he would have used it. It is inconsistent with Mark's picture of a man who closes the distance between God and humanity; who responds with warmth and passion to the needs of others on a direct, individual basis; who connects with those regarded as irredeemable; who gives hope by showing that people and their circumstances can change. Moreover, triage conflicts with the Good News that God's resources are not limited, but 'Enough for all, enough for each; Enough for evermore,' in Charles Wesley's words. It is therefore alien to the very foundation of Jesus' thinking. Jesus saw himself as the Shepherd of the flock. All the sheep were hungry, and he was convinced that God would provide the means to feed them all.

A fifth option – and another way of focusing or targeting the resources – would have been to invest them in a single person, or a couple of people, and charge them with discovering or generating a plenty which would be 'enough' for all. This is the way that people often deal with scarcity. The group entrusts its limited resources to a single person, or to a few people, in the hope that the chosen one/s will return to save or resupply the group, or, if that is impossible, that they will carry the life of the whole group forward in some other fashion. The group invests its resources – and its hope – in these representatives, on the grounds that they are the people able to make best use of the resources.

Families and communities use this strategy as a means of survival, or as a way of improving their quality of life. People living in poverty may invest heavily in the education of their children, or equip a relative who seeks better-paid work in another part of the country, or another part of the world. The more desperate the situation of the sending community, the more they may invest in those selected – not only their money, but also their hopes for more life, or indeed any life at all. The chosen ones become the saviours of the group. They will either return to lift the community out of the mire, or they will carry its values and vision into the future. So, relatives working abroad send money home, and children are sent on long, lonely journeys out of war zones, bearing their families' deep, fierce will to live.

From a purely rational point of view, if Jesus was serious in his desire to keep the crowd together and feed everyone in it, then this last option is the only one which might have worked. He could have sent a couple of the disciples away, giving them the available food to strengthen them for the journey and charging them to bring back the means to feed everyone else. Strategies like this enable groups to live when they would otherwise die.

A group will only take this course, however, when it has no other means of alleviating its situation. It is a high-risk strategy of last resort, because there is no guarantee of success, and if the chosen ones fail, there is nothing in reserve. Those who are sent can feel burdened by responsibility, trapped under the weight of other people's expectations and guilty if they survive when others do not; while those who are left behind may sink into a state of dependency and despair. The strategy carries the implicit message that they are less viable and less valuable because they are incapable of saving themselves. In other words, that they are expendable.

Jesus takes a different route by rejecting all these possibilities. Furthermore, he seems to understand that the distribution of food within a group reflects the manner in which other resources, and other forms of power, are structured and deployed, both within the group and outside it. The position of an individual in the food chain is an important clue to the extent to which that person is valued. Moreover, the way that the food chain is organized reflects the group's collective vision of who they are, who belongs, who does not, how the group functions, what matters to its members, and why.

With this in mind, Jesus demonstrates how resources are distributed within the kingdom of God. He remains faithful to the vision of God's kingdom as the feast to which all are invited, and where all are welcomed, included and fed. He assumes that this vision shows us God's intention; that God is actively realizing this purpose, and will therefore honour any act that collaborates with it. In short, he trusts that God will be God: that if he, Jesus, acts as if God's promise is true, then God will respond by making the impossible possible.

Jesus rejects any option which does not address the need of the crowd as a whole. He pursues a 'whole body' response to the problem even though this requires him to think, believe and act in a manner which is irrational. He keeps faith with what he believes to be the fundamental principles of God's relationship with humanity: that every individual is valuable, and that every aspect of the human personality has worth.

By acting as he does, Jesus declares that he will feed them as whole people; and that he intends to feed them all.

Question: How do I actually deploy my personal resources? What does this tell me about my priorities? How do I justify these choices to myself? What do these justifications tell me about what is important to me?

Reflection: 1 Samuel 1.1–8. The distribution of food reflects the realities of power within a family.

> I need to know
> that there is bread
> for the journey.
> Bread for today;
> the assurance
> of bread tomorrow.
> Bread for me;
> and for those
> who depend upon me.
> Bread for every appetite,
> every desire;
> for all in the house,
> and all who come;
> Bread for vision,
> guidance, courage,
> hope.
>
> We need to know
> that we will have bread
> for our journey,
> so that we can face the road
> and all its challenges;
> so that we can take this step,
> do the job before us,
> love one another.
> Live.

Making it real

There comes a moment in any creative process when we must act as if the vision is real. Our actions turn the idea of abundance into specific forms: a cake, a new set of bookshelves, coffee with a friend, a family outing, an album of favourite photographs, an act of worship for Trinity Sunday. Through our actions, abundance becomes a blessing we can use; a bounty we can experience; a richness we can enjoy.

This is not always easy, but it is always *possible* – that is the promise. Jesus showed that it is so, and he demonstrated how it is done. As we act to make the vision real, we are keeping faith with the gospel. We are believing the

Good News, not only with our heads, but with our hearts and hands as well. The journey of faith is a path of increasing creativity. It is the same process, the same Spirit, which enables us to have faith in ourselves, one another and God, and to act as if the richness of God can be realized by the actions we take. This is why the blessings that the Spirit brings are called gifts and fruits. They are the abundant life of God made visible in forms we can see, hear, smell, touch and taste.

As we take action, the vision of abundance – this vague, ephemeral, intangible glimpse that we have caught with our imagination – becomes personal. We are children of the Creator, made in the image of our creative God, and as such, we are called to be creative as God is creative, to be filled with God's creative Spirit. God's blessing upon us is this very ability to be fruitful, to multiply and to fill the earth by seeing visions, dreaming dreams and taking action to make them real. It is with our plans and projects and schemes that we subdue, organize and order the material world, its creatures and its resources.

The promise becomes real, first of all, to us. We see that the plenty of God is indeed available and accessible for everyone. It moves from being an impersonal, general belief to a way of investing in myself and a way of investing myself in others, and in a greater cause. It makes sense to me, and makes sense for me, of who I am, where I am and what is happening around me. It connects what I see with what I think and how I feel, what I do and how I do it. It feeds me and fills me. My belief is given particular form – in me.

This way of being creative is also a venture of faith, however. At some point we have to give our idea of abundant life a particular shape, using who we are and what we have in our hands, here and now. We have to fix it, pin it down. This involves making choices, excluding all other options and facing the possibility that we will make a mistake, maybe even fail. So taking action can be hard, so hard that we dread it, or go to great lengths to avoid it, since to act is to go beyond the point of no return.

I cut up magazines, collecting images that interest me: landscapes, faces, clothes, objects, shapes, colours, textures. I sort them without stopping to analyse them: which go together? Which ones connect? Which share a style, colour, shape or theme? I try various combinations. Which work best? Each group goes into a plastic pocket, each pocket into a loose-leaf file. As the file grows, I put the pockets into a sequence, following my instincts. Do I grade them by scale or theme or colour or 'atmosphere'? Do I move from the light into the dark and back again, or vice versa?

The collection is a form of abundance. I play, sorting and re-sorting, adding new images, deleting others, discovering new connections and combinations.

As I pay attention, I am fed, excited, challenged and inspired. The possibilities seem to be endless. But if I go on playing, the effect begins to wear off. I get bored.

When that happens, I glue pictures into a scrapbook. Now I am no longer experimenting. I am making something of the images: fixing their potential in a form I can use. This process has a different sort of excitement, and its own anxiety. It forces me to choose. Which images? Which combination? Which arrangement? On which page? In which sequence? Is there an overall scheme? If so, what is it and what does it mean? As I choose, I am selecting one possibility and excluding others. If I regret a choice, I have to live with the consequences. The results are rough, haphazard, often far from perfect, but as the pictures go into the notebook, I find myself jotting down thoughts for an event, ideas for a sermon, the kernel of a story, the first line of a poem.

Taking action is scary; it can make the whole process of 'fixing' abundant life so awesome that we prefer not to get into it at all. But the vision of abundance alone will not feed us forever. At some point we have to stop generating ideas, playing with possibilities and dreaming our dreams, and fix the abundance in some form or other. If we don't, we lose momentum and the work suffers. Fixing the abundance can give us fresh impetus. One form of abundant life can inspire another, and the forms can engage and interact, allowing us to communicate the promise, the plenty and the potential we have seen.

Ultimately, if we wish to share our vision, it has to become a meal, a song, a play, a party, a hug. It will only be life-giving if it is made personal, practical and material; if someone can see it, hear it and touch it; if it takes a form which can be experienced and enjoyed; which meets the need of the moment and makes sense to us as whole people. To convey life to another, the form has to 'match' the need with a reasonable degree of precision. It has to 'scratch where we are itching'; it has to 'hit the spot'.

This is how Jesus acts, throughout his ministry. People are keen to hear his message, so he teaches them many things. They are like sheep without a shepherd, so he leads them. They are hungry, so he feeds them. His actions – not just on this one occasion, but on every occasion – forge the link between what God wants to give and what people long to receive.

He makes it look so easy, but we spend our whole lives learning how to act as he does, with the same blend of simple faith and fertile creativity. The journey of faith is a lifelong quest to make life abundant in the ways which matter. It is the human quest for the life-giving treasure. This is why we venture out on mission, why mission is endlessly challenging, and why it is a creative process. We work towards the meeting of every kind of human need. Faith is the process of creating abundant life for all.

Question: In what ways do I 'fix' abundant life in specific forms? What are the anxieties, hesitations and doubts that I face as I do so?

Reflection: Genesis 1.26–28. Humanity is made in the image of the Creator, with the ability to be 'fruitful' and to 'multiply' in every sense.

> There is an abundance for others,
> but there is also abundance for me:
> a place where I am given energy,
> resilience, life; a room of my own,
> even if it is only in my mind;
> a space where I am seen, heard,
> received, understood and welcome;
> regardless of how I am feeling,
> regardless of what I have done.
> This place revives me, feeds me, heals me.
> Here I discover what I need to do next.
> And the strength with which to do it.
>
> There is an abundance for others,
> and there is an abundance for me:
> resources to play with, a chest to unpack,
> containing all I will ever need;
> images for vision, ideas to build me up,
> tools I can use;
> glimpses of how these things are connected
> to other parts of my life, to other peoples' lives,
> to all that has brought me to this place,
> and to one or more of my futures.
>
> There is an abundance for others,
> and there is an abundance for me,
> simply to be enjoyed: time to try things out;
> a space in which I can stretch my horizons,
> find the well of acceptance deepening;
> know that as I fix the plenty, here and now,
> some part of it becomes a part of me,
> and that part is mine to keep.
>
> There is an abundance for others,
> and there is abundance for me,
> so that I can gain life, give life, freely;

find the thread which leads from here
back into the world:
to continue, but with fresh vigour,
to a completion, the satisfaction of a task well done,
to another new beginning, for there is always more.

Acting as if

In the film *Indiana Jones and the Last Crusade* the hero has to face three challenges in the last stages of his hunt for the Holy Grail. Having met and overcome two of them, Jones reaches the end of a narrow tunnel to find himself on the lip of a chasm that cuts right across his path. He must go forward because he needs the life-giving power of the Grail to heal his father, who is dying of a bullet-wound. But there is no way around the obstacle. So he must cross the chasm. But how? He cannot jump the gap, for it is too wide. He cannot climb down and up the other side, for its walls are sheer and its bottom is lost in darkness. He cannot make a bridge, for he has no materials and no tools. What is he to do? After a moment of hesitation, he recognizes the nature of the challenge. 'It's a leap of faith,' he says, and, closing his eyes, steps out, into the air.

So often, the obstacle before us is an absence or lack of resources which prevents us from doing what we want to do, going where we want to go, achieving what we want to achieve. The pressure is on; the stakes are rising. We need to act, and act soon, but it also matters how we act: that we take others with us, that we remain faithful to our highest principles, and that we make the most creative response possible. How do we move forward?

By acting as if . . . acting as if the obstacle is not there, as if we are crossing it, or walking through it, or overcoming it. Acting as if we have reached the other side.

Of course, we cannot, must not, act like this. It is impossible. We will fail, or fail others. It is a stupid idea and we will be mocked if we try it. It would be bad stewardship to do this; we would be acting irresponsibly. We will be judged, perhaps dismissed or even punished by those who can call us to account. We must not risk the things that matter most to us, or we might lose them.

Our fear magnifies both the obstacle itself and our objections. Our anxieties focus on unanswered questions. What does the action involve? Do we have the resources to take it? How will it work? Will it be effective? What will be the consequences of success? Of failure? Do the possible gains outweigh the risks? Can we alter course or amend the consequences at a later stage? How will our action be received? Can we cope with the aftermath? It is appropriate and natural to be scared if it seems we will be wasting our efforts or sacrificing ourselves or putting ourselves in the way of harm. The question is whether we allow our fear to make our decision for us; whether we act from fear or act against it; whether we recognize our fear and acknowledge it but go ahead despite it.

Rationally, this is where the journey ends. This is where we cut our losses and settle for what we have, rather than continuing to pursue an impossible dream. In that case, Indiana Jones turns around, walks back down the tunnel and comforts the father he cannot save. Perhaps he dies fighting the villain who shot his dad; or perhaps he avoids a confrontation with forces too strong for him, abandons his father, and escapes from the Temple of the Grail with anyone who has the wit or the luck to follow. He is scarred by his terrible loss, but he lives to fight another day. However, the Grail is forever beyond his reach, undiscovered and unclaimed. He will never experience the 'more life', the 'better life' it promises.

A rational way of thinking would lead Jesus to concentrate his resources, give them to a couple of the apostles, and send them off to find enough food to feed the crowd. If he explained his thinking to the crowd, they might have accepted this, especially if he appealed to their hearts as well as their heads. But the message of the action would have been that while the feast of the kingdom is a wonderful vision, here and now we can operate only within the limitations of human power. Here and now, we can only work with what we are given. There is not enough to go around, and there is very little we can do about it.

To 'act as if' is to step out into the air, like Indiana Jones. We act as if we know what we are doing, even though we don't, as if there is a path, even though we cannot see it. We act as if what we are doing is not only possible, but the right thing to do, even though our heads tell us it is not. We act as if we can cope regardless of the consequences, even though we know what this might cost us. In short, we act from faith, rather than from fear. We act as if God's promises are true. We act as if God is with us, and will keep faith with us, whatever happens.

Jesus acts as if his vision is true. He keeps faith with the vision of God's kingdom as a life-giving feast to which all are invited. He acts as if the bread in his hands is enough to achieve this. He receives the bread, gives thanks, breaks it and orders its distribution. He acts as if the meal is ready, the table is laid and a vast banquet is spread before him. He acts as if the crowd are invited guests, every one of them welcomed, and honoured.

By acting in this way, Jesus draws everyone into his vision of the world and how it works. He encourages them to go along with him, one step at a time. Perhaps they wonder what on earth he is doing, whether he has taken leave of his senses, where he is leading them. But they trust him enough to follow him. He has made the vision real for them in so many other ways; why not in this way too?

Question: Is there a situation in which I am being challenged to 'act as if' an obstacle can be overcome? What are my anxieties about doing so?

Reflection: 1 Kings 19.9–13. Elijah realizes that the overwhelming power of his enemies cannot snuff out the 'still small voice' of God.

> Living God, everlasting Creator,
> Lord of the ends of the earth:
> your sight covers and comprehends all things,
> your power and provision sustain everything created;
> yet you do not grow fragile or fearful.
> Uphold me in faith,
> protect me when I am exhausted.
> Show me how
> you give power to the weak,
> and strength to the powerless.
> As I pay attention to your promises,
> may my confidence be renewed.
> Let me launch myself on outspread wings,
> riding the air like an eagle;
> Let me run for miles without wearying;
> let me find your road through the wild.
>
> (based on Isaiah 40.28b–31)

The longest stride

Jesus has acted in faith from the very beginning of the process, but now, like Indiana Jones, it is as though he steps out into the air. He breaks the bread and orders it to be distributed amongst the people. It is a crazy, irrational, illogical step; the longest stride.

The rational response to shortage is to concentrate our resources, deploying them where they will have the greatest effect, thus maximizing and making best use of their life-giving power. But Jesus does the opposite. Having taken the bread and fish into his hands, he fragments them. Of all the options open to him, this is the only one which allows him to keep faith with his vision, and yet, what does it accomplish?

Instead of concentrating and focusing the power of the food, he dissipates it, rendering it ineffective. Whole, the bread and fish might have fed someone, now they are not enough to feed anyone. Broken into fragments, given out as crumbs, the bread no longer has the power to fill an empty belly or feed a starving soul, because, in a sense, it is no longer there. Essentially, he has removed their last hope of using the available resources to feed themselves, and destroyed what little power he had. He has given it away.

Jesus' action is a paradox. He acts as if God's vision is true. But his action does not – cannot – achieve what he wants to achieve. In itself, it does not – cannot – feed the crowd. It is not 'enough'. It is a purely symbolic act. A gesture. It does not – cannot – take him towards his goal in any practical manner. Indeed, it does not appear to take them forward at all. It does not appear to achieve anything worthwhile, that makes a difference. Arguably, it makes matters worse.

The step beyond our limitations is the scariest step of all. Knocking on that door. Making that phone call. Signing that form. Writing that cheque. Sending that card. Posting that letter. Walking into that interview. Taking that exam. Inquiring about that course, that job, that holiday. Nevertheless, we take it, even though our knees are shaking, even though we feel sick, even though we have been awake half the night. We choose to act from faith, rather than fear.

Indiana Jones steps off the cliff, but he does not fall. Incredibly, his foot lands on solid ground. As he staggers, reorienting himself and regaining his balance, the camera pans around and we can see that he is standing on a narrow strip of rock. There is a bridge, so cunningly camouflaged that it could not be seen until he committed himself and stepped onto it, until he went beyond the point of no return.

Our 'leap of faith' may feel huge and dramatic, but often it is not. We take it, trembling, and afterwards we know that it is not enough. Beforehand, we wondered whether it would achieve anything, and afterwards, we are still wondering. It seems that we have scarcely moved at all. We have stepped off the cliff and we are left hanging there, suspended over the abyss, too frightened to look down. This is very discouraging. Perhaps we have got it wrong. Perhaps we have not achieved anything – will never achieve anything – at all.

The trouble is that acting in faith does not always produce immediate results. A single leap of faith is not always enough to get us to the other side of the chasm. Some ravines are wider than others. Some limitations require more effort to circumvent or overcome. Some obstacles bite back. Sometimes we have to step out in faith again and again and again.

At this point, a sceptic will suggest that our action has been purely symbolic, a gesture – brave, ambitious, the act of a visionary, and fine in theory, perhaps, but ultimately no good at all. The suggestion is that we are play-acting, that what we have attempted is all appearance without substance; that what we have offered is nothing masquerading as something: a pretence; a charade.

Many acts of faith are indeed symbolic. It is unfortunate that we have to use that word, because these days we use symbolic to mean empty, impractical, meaningless, worthless and so on. And there is some truth in this definition. A symbolic action is personal, practical, material and specific, and so it looks real, but usually it is not enough, in itself, to reach the goal. It indicates that a life-giving process is occurring, and it is a step in that process, but it is not enough, by itself, to complete the process. More is required.

For example, to send a bunch of flowers to someone who is ill is a symbolic action. We give flowers or fruit, chocolates or teddy bears as symbols of abundant life, but our gift is not enough to make the sick person well. Our gift highlights the fact that the life-giving process of healing is happening, and it tells the recipient that we want to encourage that process. Our action does not complete that process, however. More is required: rest, medical treatment, good food, prayer, a positive mental attitude.

Every time I preside at Holy Communion, blessing bread and wine and distributing a little to each person, I engage in symbolic action. Bread and wine symbolize the abundant life of God. By distributing the elements, I declare that the life of God is given – graciously, generously and freely – as bread for the journey we make together through the world. But the life-giving power is not in the bread and wine. And even if it is, a mouthful does not make a meal. More is required: the making of a life of faith through many individual acts of faith, love, hope and prayer.

Marking the walls of the Ministry of Defence with ash in the sign of the cross is a symbolic action. The ashes express our awareness that our attempts to defend ourselves cost others their lives. The action indicates that the life-giving process of peace-making is occurring, but the marks do not alter government policy. More is required: discussion, advocacy, campaigning, lobbying, voting, action in Parliament and its committees, and new legislation.

Our 'leaps of faith' are often small actions which we rightly call symbolic, and about which we might ask, quite justifiably: what do we gain? The answer, in one sense, is 'little or nothing'. Such actions point to a life-giving process; they may even function as a form of shorthand, summarizing the process as a whole. But they do not complete it. They are not, in themselves 'enough' to meet the need.

Do we say then, that symbolic actions such as these are worthless? Not at all. Each one 'fixes' the promise of abundant life in a particular form. Each one claims that such life is available, accessible, attainable – here and now – despite all the evidence to the contrary. Each one asserts the existence of a bridge from where we are to where we want to be. Each one is a small step in the right direction across that bridge, over the ravine to the other side. Each one closes the gap between the vibrant fullness of all that God wants to give and our readiness to receive.

A symbolic action will never be enough in itself to take us to the other side of the chasm. It does not have the power to heal the sick, feed the hungry, create peace between nations. But our symbolic actions have immense value because they 're-present' the life-giving relationships and processes needed to bring about such a change. They remind us that such processes exist, and that we can use them. They remind us that every creative, compassionate, life-giving process is made up of many tiny acts of faith, taken one after another.

The trouble is, of course, that any one of those acts can seem like the 'longest stride', a step too huge and scary to take; and also, at the same time, too small and weak to matter. This is another reason why they are 'leaps of faith'. From beginning to end, they only make sense from a faith perspective. We need faith to make them, and faith to continue believing in them. They are steps on a 'way' of faith. Each one asserts our faith in the power of life to bring about a profound transformation in others and in ourselves. With each one, we choose life rather than death; we assert that fear has not yet overwhelmed us, and that it need never do so.

Question: Are there contexts in which I would take a small step forward – if I thought it would be 'worth it'? Are there situations in which I have hesitated to act because the only possible action seems only symbolic? What would I do if I was not afraid of wasting time or looking foolish?

Reflection: Exodus 14.10–16. Do not be afraid. God will act on your behalf.

Playing, exploring,
failing and trying again,
we discover that failure
need not destroy us;
that we can allow ourselves
to be less than perfect,
sufficient, wonderful,
all-knowing,
because we are more
than our mistakes.

Our sins, however grievous,
do not define who we are,
and so they cannot
annihilate us.

Our helplessness
does not define us,
because we are more
than our power,
or our lack of it;
and God looks on us
with love.

Only God defines us.
God, who made us
looks upon us
only with love.

Only God defines us,
excavating the divine image
from amongst our frailties
and falls.

Only God defines us.
Believing this,
we can step away from the familiar,
in the care of One
who knows the unknown.

The meeting of extremes

Jesus' 'way' of faith is 'another road' where a simple action – a small, purely 'symbolic' gesture – becomes a means of 'closing the gap' between the abundant life of God and the human condition in all its diversity, glory and grief. And it is this meeting of extremes which gives the action, and the moment, its power.

In all sorts of contexts, energy is created by the meeting of things which are separate, different, contrasting, even opposed. As they are brought together, they generate energy. As they connect, they interact, building tension, excitement and power.

A thunderstorm is created when droplets of warm water rub against crystals of ice in the atmosphere. Contrasting colours freshen a palette and bring a picture alive. A sudden, unexpected discord generates excitement in music. Some relationships thrive on fighting and making up again. A warm current in the cold ocean serves as a highway for predators and prey. In football, the fiercest rivalries are between teams from the same city. And in any workplace, family, church or discipline, the most vicious arguments – or the coldest silences – develop between those who are repelled by one another but forced into proximity without the skills or strategies to manage their interaction creatively.

Extremes do not meet easily, because they are simply that – extremes. Their coming together is often loud, vibrant, jarring, chaotic. It is not automatically creative. There are ways to make the encounter fruitful, but we have to search for them. They require investment, work, flexibility, negotiation and risk. This is not a task for those who want quick results or an easy ride. Extremes can be aligned so that they work together, but the effort required to keep them so means that the relationship is fragile and inherently unstable. The meeting has to be finely tuned, like a caress or a kiss or dance. To be successful, we require energy, enthusiasm, experience and expertise, but in the long term the most important quality we need is endurance: the determination to continue the adventure and an openness to all that can be discovered at every stage.

Extremes can meet as part of a greater whole, but because their encounters are so volatile, this 'whole' cannot be fixed in time or space. It cannot be too tightly structured, closely controlled or strictly organized. We cannot expect it to last. It does not have a permanent form. It has to remain fluid, dynamic, on the move. It has to be a process: an inquiry, a project, a romance, a quest, a treasure hunt, a journey.

The clashes between England and Australia can be made real – that is personal, practical, material and specific – through the devotion of each country to the game of cricket. But each fixture is transient: only lasting as long as a game, or a series. The clash is contained by the process of play and the rules which govern that process, but beyond that, everything is fluid, variable, dynamic. Anything can happen, so there is everything to play for. Australia may have won The Ashes this time, but there is always another tour!

The meeting of opposites is like a story. While the story lasts, the extremes can continue to interact, like characters in a romance or a thriller. The dialogue may be passionate and the action explosive, but because the interaction occurs as part of a narrative – a process – it can be contained and directed towards a greater goal. And within this arc, the extremes can meet as often as is necessary or desirable. They can continue to interact even though doing so requires them to accept discomfort, think on their feet, undergo change, take risks, overcome obstacles, and work through their fears.

Question: Where am I caught up in a 'meeting of extremes'? What skills or qualities would help me manage the encounter more creatively? Where might I find them? What would I like to achieve?

Reflection: Ecclesiastes 2.24 – 3.15. The author sees how actions and processes which are opposed to one another are nevertheless contained within the purposes of God, which is where we should look for permanence.

When life is brought
to the point of death,
song to the point
of silence –

When mercy appeals
to judgement,
and hope is ground
by the stone of despair –

When love reaches out
to hatred, and peace
steals into the midst
of war –

That is when the dancers
pause,
and in the space
between one heartbeat
and the next,
there is a stillness.

If you look beyond
the leading edge of light,
you can see
the shadows move.

It is in turning to face
the fear which brushes
our spine,
and raising our gaze
to look into the eyes
of our enemy,
that we halt
the juggernaut.

If you look beyond
the leading edge of light,
you can see
that the shadows
are alive.

Chapter 7
The School of Faith

It is said that Jesus loved the crowds who followed him, and that is true. No one could have cared for them as he cared for them – feeding the hungry, healing the sick, calming the fearful, freeing those who were tormented by forces they could not understand or control – no one, I tell you, could have done these things for so many and for so long if he had not loved the crowd. He saw them as sheep without a shepherd. It made him angry that no one else seemed to be bothered about them, so he travelled all over, worked long days, cut short his rest. Because he loved them. He loved them as individuals. He loved them all.

But it is not true, as some have said, that he used the crowd as a platform, as a means of building his own power. A lot of people expected him to do that, and some of us hoped he would challenge the collaborators, even the Roman Empire, but that was never what he was about. No, he never saw the crowd as a means to an end. He did not even try to get them to follow him, most of the time. If they got the message: if they saw that God had faith in them: that was enough.

He used to say that the crowd was like a patch of varied ground, and that a teacher was like a sower, scattering seed. The Good News takes root in the unlikeliest places, and in good soil it yields a hundredfold. But you can never tell. Some people are keen at first, but do not endure. It is as if the gospel becomes strangled by other things. And so, when people sought him out and hung on his every word and followed him around the country, he was pleased that they were encouraged, renewed and inspired. But he did not feed on their adulation. He did not need it. He knew how to detach himself. At an early stage he learned how to let them go. How to walk away.

At first, we thought this was because he lacked ambition. But, no, it was that he understood what the crowd is like. Its limitations, if you will. He knew that you can't build anything durable or permanent on the back of a crowd. Crowds are transient, volatile, fickle, perilous. They come and they go. And in his own way, Jesus was very ambitious, but what he wanted was very specific – narrower, but also much deeper and more far-reaching, than any of us recognized at the time. You see, it was his great desire, not just to proclaim the kingdom of God, but to bring it into being. He believed that if we have faith in ourselves, in one another, and in God, we make it real.

And so he founded a school of faith. It met wherever he was staying and consisted of whoever was around at the time: friends, followers, patrons and disciples. Small, fluid, overlapping groups, eating together, staying together, travelling together. We were varied in every way: men and women, young and old, rich and poor, individuals, couples, whole extended families. We came from all social backgrounds, all parts of the country, and every political faction. Some he picked out, deliberately, for a specific role; others chose themselves and did whatever they could. Some went on the road with him regularly; some remained in their homes and provided hospitality when he was in the neighbourhood; some did a bit of both at different times; yet more hung around the fringes, dipping in and out. But we all had one thing in common. We stayed with him, and we stayed to learn.

Jesus understood that the obstacles to faith are many, varied, subtle and tenacious. He did not tell people they *must* believe, nor *what* they should believe. Rather, he saw his task as being to *help* them believe. Believe in themselves. Believe in one another. Believe in God. For him, spreading the Good News was about inspiring faith, generating faith, building faith, sustaining faith, resourcing faith.

He had loads of ideas, yes, but he didn't want us to believe them because he told us to, or because God commanded it, nor even because they might be true. He wanted us to believe them because this was how we received forgiveness, healing, hope. When you have a bit of faith in yourself, it brings you alive. It gives you more energy, a greater quality of life. It makes you more loving, more generous, more creative. That's why he wanted us to have faith – for our sakes. Never for his.

But his ideas are so radical, you can't take them in at once. It takes time to see what he means, to learn how it works, to take it in and think it through and make it your own. It has to become part of you so that it starts to shape the way you look at things, the way you think about what is going on, the way you feel about yourself, the way you speak and act. You have to let it form you, or re-form you, until you live it from the inside out; until it becomes natural, a habit, instinctive. And then somehow, somewhere along the line you find yourself teaching others how to do it, too.

That's the bit I struggled with – that he saw us all as capable of being like him. That he was teaching us how to have faith so that we could do the things he did. So that one day, when he was gone, we could take over and continue the work. I think that's what he had in mind more or less from the beginning: that there would come a time when – one way or another – he would have to leave us. That there would never be enough time for him to spread the gospel to all who needed to hear it. But he trusted that he had time enough for this:

to form a group of people who would learn to live by faith; who would encourage each other in preaching and practising the Good News; and who would teach others to do the same. That was us, his school of faith.

So he showed us what he expected us to do, and got us doing it. From the outset we were involved in his work with the crowd. Some of his favourite stories we heard many, many times. But he also sent us out to retell those stories, and to create our own; to spread the Good News that God loves us and has faith in us; and to help people face and deal with their problems. It was daunting, demanding, exhausting work, but there were some memorable encounters. Some incidents stay with you. Some faces you never forget.

And then, when the day's work was over, and we gathered together wherever we were staying to share a meal, we would go over it all again. As soon as the prayer of blessing was said and the food was served, the conversation would start, and before long everyone would be pitching in. Unpacking everything that had occurred and chewing it over. Who had said what. Who had done what. What had happened next. And in the middle of it all, someone would ask a question of Jesus – what had he meant when he said this – why had he done this or that thing – and then we would be off. An explanation, a joke, a story. More questions. A discussion that often became an argument as people got heated. If he was lucky, Jesus got something to eat before it got too deep, because once we got going we were often at it until midnight.

Jesus took these sessions very seriously. He put a lot of energy into them, even when it had been a long day. He gave us his time and attention, even when he had so much else on his mind. Because this was when he taught us, cared for us, and guided us, as his disciples and as his friends. This was when he showed us how faith help us do what God wants us to do – and how it helps us with our personal concerns, too. This was when he listened to our experience, helped us examine it, and enabled us to see what we had learned from it. This was when we were free to question him, argue with him, disagree with him. Often, we would wrestle with an issue until we reached a dead end, and then he would suggest a fresh way of looking at the problem, and – hey! – we'd come out the other side.

It was during these times that he fed us, schooled us, discipled us. Of course, he was teaching us all the time; he was our example of what it means to live a life of faith. But it was during those informal teaching sessions – the Lord's Suppers, as we called them – that he helped us explore what we were learning, integrate it and reinforce it into something consistent and coherent. So despite their informality and confusion, they were vital. Intensive, searching and demanding, yes. But also life-giving: to him and to us. They energized everybody.

Jesus himself saw them as symbolizing and celebrating the life we shared. He enjoyed his food. He loved a party. He had his own special way of giving the blessing. He would take bread, give thanks for it, then break it up and share it out, as if he wanted to make sure we all got our share of the feast. He did not want any of us to have anything less than the abundance God desired for us.

He had the same attitude regardless of how much food was actually on the table. In fact sometimes there wasn't much to eat at all, but he always broke bread as if there was a banquet spread before him. He welcomed what was given, even when it was not enough. He gave thanks for it, even when it was not enough. He shared bread and wine as if it would meet our every need.

It was a form of play-acting, I suppose. And yet it summed up everything he did. This was his attitude to everything and everyone. This was what he was about. And I see now that he used those simple gestures as a way of getting us to remember the heart of his teaching. Look, he was saying, this is how we discover the life we were meant to live; the fullness of life God intends for us. This is how we live lives of faith and hope and love. This is how we enjoy the abundant life of God.

The gesture of perseverance

Having broken the bread, Jesus gives it to the disciples to lay before the people, and divides the two fish amongst them all. In John's Gospel, the division and distribution of the food is depicted as a single act, which Jesus controls from start to finish. Mark shows us two separate decisions: the decision to *act* and the decision to *persist* until all are fed. Furthermore, he wants us to see that the disciples are participants throughout; serving Jesus by serving the people.

The fourth step of the creative process is the gesture of perseverance: our willingness to continue the process until it is complete. Following the high drama of the 'leap of faith'; the decision to keep going can look, sound and feel like a tedious slog. Consequently, this part of the process tends to be played down, even ignored. We prefer to imagine the Holy Spirit making large sweeping actions, not crossing the T's and dotting the I's down amongst the small print. But you only have to watch the credits rolling on the latest Hollywood blockbuster to realize that the 'big picture' gets onto the screen because behind the producer and the director and the headlined actors, hundreds of other people are paying attention to details essential to the creativity of the team and the success of the project. At least 90 per cent of any creative process is perspiration, rather than inspiration. Most of the faithfulness in a life of faith is expressed as patience, persistence, perseverance and endurance.

Mark knows this. His Gospel is written to help Jesus' followers live through a period of terrible upheaval and apocalyptic change (chapter 13), in the belief that those who endure to the end will be saved (13.13). Mark knows that the ways of God, or the actions of Jesus, do not always produce instant results. There is a process at work, which requires our attention. Jesus' encounters with individuals often involve persistence, either on his part, or on the part of someone else. The woman who has been suffering from haemorrhages has to brave the exposure of her private pain to receive the full measure of healing (5.25–34). Jairus has to wait before Jesus is free to attend to his dying daughter, a delay which tests his faith to the limit (5.35–43). The Syrophoenician woman argues her case to secure relief for her daughter (7.24–30). To heal a man who is deaf and who has a speech impediment Jesus must perform a sequence of actions (7.31–37). At Bethsaida, a man who is blind receives his sight in stages, after Jesus lays hands on him twice (8.22–26). And Bartimaeus has to attract Jesus' attention by calling out, repeatedly (10.46–52).

We demonstrate our faith by following Jesus (1.17; 2.14; 8.34; 10.52), by pursuing his vision of God's abundant life, and the process of making that abundance real, to the very end, because even the manner of our dying can witness to it (15.37–39). We are travelling the wilderness road with the messenger of God who prepares the way of the Lord by making his paths straight (1.2–3), an ongoing work which requires power and authority, and also a faithful, persistent attention to detail. There is a sense in which the disciples go ahead of Jesus, preparing for his entry into Jerusalem, and his celebration of the Passover (11.1–10; 14.12–16); and a sense in which Jesus goes ahead of us (6.47–51;16.6–7) to a place where we will see him. The road goes on, and we have to stay on it.

However, we cannot travel successfully by focusing on survival. The faithful persistence asked of us is more than keeping our head down during times of trouble, or sticking things out until our term of office ends, or slogging on until the work is done just to get it finished. Instead, it is assumed that while we are waiting, we are exercising patience; that while we keep going, we are continuing to pay attention; and that while we are nailing down the details, we are keeping an eye on the overall vision. Here again, mission is not about what we do, so much as how we go about it. It is the way we persevere until the task is complete which allows the task to be completed generously, creatively, compassionately.

Our example is the patience of God, who continues to reach out, creating space for a positive response even when that trust is resisted (12.1–11). A mysterious power is at work (4.26–29), capable of producing amazing growth (4.30–32), but if the process is to be fruitful, we have to put energy and effort into being 'good soil' in which the seed of God's word can grow (4.1–8, 14–20). For the disciples, this means practising the 'way' of Jesus – the 'secret' or 'mystery' of the kingdom. For the crowd, it means brooding on Jesus' parables, which contain all his teaching (4.10–12). The same key unlocks them all (4.13): the 'way' of faith: the vision of God's abundant life and the strategy Jesus taught for making that abundance real.

The seeds which grow to the point of bearing fruit are those which endure despite the demands, distractions and dangers of their context. This does not happen automatically. We flourish in adverse conditions by remembering and revisiting and refreshing the vision of abundant life for all, and repeating, as necessary, every step of Jesus' strategy. We have to keep on accepting the 'givens' of our situation; offering praise and thanks to God 'always and everywhere'; and acting as if the vision is true. Indeed, the more difficult our circumstances, the more we persist in imagining abundance for ourselves and for others; and the more we apply Jesus' 'way' to find the food, the resources, the 'more life' that will keep us going, keep us growing, keep us faithful.

The further we travel, the more that the 'way' can feed us. This is the 'secret of the kingdom'. Those who view the 'way' from outside will never understand it (4.12), but travellers find that it gives them light, like a lamp set on a stand (4.21). It reveals what is otherwise hidden (4.22–23). It refreshes the vision which makes our journey worthwhile, and reminds us of the strategy which makes it possible and productive. If we pay attention to the 'way', our investment is returned, with interest (4.24–25).

Question: Where do I need to persist with a creative process until a task is complete? Do I need to pay more attention to the details so that the process becomes more compassionate or creative? Who can I ask to help me?

Reflection: 1 Kings 19.13–21. Elijah is sent back to his task, and given Elisha to help him.

Needing space to stretch out,
draw breath, laugh, relax;
I leave the desk, the house,
the street.

Needing to let rip, hang out,
make sense of what I can,
let go of what will never

make sense at all;
I find a place where I can sit with you,
cool down, allow the world
to pass me by,
and let the sap rise[1], slowly.

Needing to pray, eat, learn, receive
the life of God,
I let a mind meet mine,
feel the pleasure of relationship,
allow the flower of my soul
to unfold and seek the sun.

Needing to establish
fresh connections,
I let myself be found,
allow myself to find you;
remind myself that I am here,
that you are here,
and that our bond
is only ever broken
to the extent
that I stop being aware of it.

You are holding me still,
even when I am far off,
running,
running away,
running away from myself,
and from you, and the conversation
we need to have
in the silence
I am avoiding
by shovelling blame
and filling the world with storm.

Walking on water

How long does the distribution take? We do not know. But all that time, we can suppose that Jesus is praying: standing back so that he can let others continue what he has begun; giving them space to work, even though he is still overseeing the process and will take all the blame if it goes wrong.

The disciples are far outside their comfort zone. Jesus has not acted as they advised him to act, but has followed his vision despite the lack of resources. So it is reasonable to assume that as they set the food before the people, they are praying too: setting their reservations to one side so that they can take this other road against their (better) judgement; offering these tiny pieces of bread even though they are such an inadequate response to the overwhelming need; paying attention to the task even though it is exposing them to the questions, the doubts, the ridicule of others.

There are times when we can only persevere with a creative process if we act like this. To be more accurate, perhaps, the process will only continue to be creative if we act like this. This is where prayer and action fuse into one. Our prayer is that we pick our way forward, as, step by step, we see how we can keep going despite our fear. Our prayer is in the way we cling to the principles Jesus has given us, wrestle with the decisions we must make; share with God all the pain and promise of remaining faithful to the path we have chosen; ask the questions we do not want to ask; turn around to look into the shadow which follows us.

The key to this prayerful proceeding is an unqualified honesty; our willingness to face exactly how we feel, even if our thoughts are barely thinkable, and to lay out all our options, including the ones we do not wish to consider. Most of us have to learn that we can be this honest with ourselves, and with God. We have to practise long and hard before we are willing to set aside the thoughts we use as a shield against the light. We do not want to see ourselves exactly as we are: we would rather believe that we are worse than we are, or better than we are. We do not like to appear naked because we are afraid that this will end any chance of God loving us, feeding us, helping us.

This way of prayer can be hard work – perhaps the hardest and most costly work we ever do – and yet it is utterly necessary that we attempt it, and that we go on attempting it. This is the true heart of the creative process: this is what it has become, what it always becomes if we wish to persevere with it: a struggle within ourselves to stay with the task as Jesus wants it done. We have to act as if Jesus knows what he is doing. We have to trust him. He is relying on us. He has faith that if we trust him, his 'way' will work in the end.

Jesus' 'way' is a journey into an ever-deepening trust. There are so many anxious or critical voices telling us that what we are doing means nothing, achieves nothing, is going nowhere. Some of those voices will be inside our own heads. They will argue that we are being irresponsible to carry on; that our action has no evidence to support it; that we are pretending, flying in the face of reality.

In a sense, that is exactly what is going on. Mark tells us how, when the five thousand have been fed, Jesus remains behind on the mountainside, praying, while the disciples take the boat and set out across the lake. The wind is against them, and though they strain at the oars, they make little headway. In the early hours of the morning, Jesus comes to them, walking on the lake. He intends to pass them by, but they believe they are seeing a ghost, and cry out, terrified. 'Take heart, it is I; do not be afraid,' he says. He gets into the boat with them, and the wind ceases. Mark comments: 'And they were utterly astounded, for they did not understand about the loaves, but their hearts were hardened' (6.51–52).

What had they failed to understand? Is Mark saying that because Jesus was able to feed the crowd the disciples should not have been surprised to discover that he could do other amazing things as well, or is he saying that what Jesus did with the loaves shows us the true nature of the 'way': that it carries us along, allowing us to be creative, compassionate and generous in difficult circumstances, but that as we proceed it feels as if we are walking on water. We are not sure what is supporting us; all we know is that the process is allowing us to make progress where we would not normally be able to go at all.

If so, then this story shows us the Spirit at work. It makes the dynamic visible. The dynamic or energy can work because at every step, Jesus acts in faith. By contrast, the disciples are overawed and uneasy, and then, as they strain to make progress against an adverse wind, they become afraid that everything – the whole world, even God – is against them. So when they see what Jesus is doing, they are terrified. They think they are seeing a ghost, when what they are seeing is a spiritual reality of a rather different kind. They are seeing the life-giving power which enables Jesus to get from where he is to where he wants to be.

Significantly, if we look at the story from Jesus' point of view, it begins in prayer and ends in peace. Perhaps recognizing that the disciples have had enough for one day, he sends them away while he dismisses the crowd. Was this a straightforward matter, or did it take some time for him to detach himself from their gratitude and interest and enthusiasm? Anyway, he says farewell and climbs the mountain, walking into solitude, stillness, silence. He is alone now, alone with himself, with all that he is carrying, and with God.

He knows that his disciples are having problems with the 'way'. They have learned how to apply it in personal encounters but they need to learn that it will work for them in much larger contexts too, when the need is huge and every circumstance is against them. He wants to show them how it will carry them forward, whatever the scale of the task and however fierce the opposition, if they are willing to face their fear. He wants to go ahead of them, walking across the lake to show them that this process will take them wherever they need to go. It is fear which is their enemy, the only enemy. He speaks to encourage them: to show them that they do not need to be afraid.

The 'way' itself will carry them through, if only they focus on the next step of the process, rather than on all the things they dread. All the power is in the process. It is the process which leads us, step by step, to peace.

Question: Where do I feel that I am 'walking on water'? What am I afraid will happen if I carry on? What needs to change before I can let go of this fear?

Reflection: Psalm 107.1–3, 23–32, 43. God meets us in the midst of storm, and gives us quiet.

Drawn to the story,
intrigued by the dream,
attracted by the promise,
I long to believe
without actually being sure.
This belief I hold
with part of myself
is so often undermined.
Deep down, I struggle to believe
that God actually means it,
that God actually means us,
that God actually means me.
Perhaps I want it to be true too much.
I can hold the thought
in general terms,
meaning everyone else,
the special people,
the genuine Christians,
the holy ones.
But I am always hoping
no one will ask me
too many questions,
look too deep into my eyes,
find me out.
Even now, after all these years,
it is still hard to believe
he means me.
Me. Here. Now.
As I am.
Here. Now.

Living from faith, not fear

What we long for is forbidden to us or snatched from us or spoiled for us by our fear. The structures and forces which oppose us are all built on fear and powered by fear: the fear in other people, yes, but matched by the fear within us. Even when we are set free by our circumstances, we can remain imprisoned by our fear of all that lies beyond that open door.

Fear is a signal. It tells us that action is needed and that our energies are being gathered to take that action. There are times when it is appropriate to be afraid, and times when our 'nerves' give us an edge which we can use to improve our performance. Fear is a useful tool, providing that it is working for us and not against us.

We fear so many things. Making a beginning. The unknown. Change – even a change we long to see. We can be afraid of not having enough, or doing enough to accomplish the task in hand. We fear choices and consequences. We can be afraid that people will criticize us and judge us; that we will fail. We can fear that we will not be in time, or that we will be too late. We can be terrified of what we might discover if we really look – at ourselves, or at others.

Fear becomes our enemy when we become aware of a threat but sense that we cannot deal with it. This may be because we cannot see it clearly, or identify it. We may know what it is, but do not know how to protect all that we love, or we do not know where to start, or we cannot take any action yet because the time is not right. There may be simply nothing we can do. If we cannot act to help ourselves, the energies we have gathered cannot be deployed. They churn around within us, creating turmoil. Being afraid is unpleasant. Fear makes us feel bad about ourselves, our circumstances, other people, life itself.

Fear occurs in many degrees and wears many disguises: apathy, lethargy, denial, evasion, deceit, exhaustion, depression, persistent ill-health, anxiety, a tendency to worry or over-work or over-organize, jealousy, greed, envy, lust, a need to control people and situations, arrogance, anger, bitterness, bullying, suspicion, abuse, self-harm, violence.

We develop all manner of strategies to deal with our fear. We deny it is there, refuse to face it. We delay making a decision or taking action. We distract ourselves with fantasy or escapist literature. We drown it in sleep, sex, sugar, alcohol or drugs. We sink into a stupor, becoming depressed, apathetic, ill, or we go to the other extreme, becoming hyperactive, bad-tempered, impatient, frustrated, violent. We may develop a corrosive cynicism. We may try to control what is going on inside us by managing our diet of food or other types of 'input'. We may try to control what is going on around us by becoming excessively neat and tidy. We may try to control other people by imposing our rules upon them.

We all have our ways of coping with fear, but some strategies are more helpful than others, and all of them, used too often or pushed to an extreme, become unhealthy for us, our relationships and even society as a whole. On the other hand, we must learn how to handle our fear, because unless we do, it will work against us, colouring the way we see ourselves and the world. It can sabotage our happiness, undermine our achievements, destroy our blessings and wound those who care for us. And yet, we will never 'grow out of' being afraid, because fear is a useful signal, necessary to our safety and well-being. So we need to find ways of managing our fear: ways which allow it to serve us, so that, to a greater extent, we are masters of our fear, rather than constantly feeling that our negative emotions are mastering us.

One way in which the gospel can help us is by teaching us how to live from faith rather than fear.[2] We can learn ways of seeing the world which give us a greater measure of confidence and courage, and learn how to handle difficult situations so that the outcome is better for us and better for others, too.

The good news is this: faith is possible. Imagine there is a treasury of wonderful resources held in reserve for the very moment you need them. An ever-flowing fountain of life. A vast still pool of tranquillity, harmony and peace. A bubbling, bottomless well of mercy, understanding, forgiveness and love. An ever-expanding chest of brilliant ideas. An inexhaustible fund of wisdom, knowledge and common sense. A rugged, sturdy store of purpose, determination and resilience. A bright, sparkling stream of hope. Imagine you have the key to this treasury; that you can open the storehouse whenever you like, and take from it whatever you need, as much as you need.

The good news is this: faith is possible. Faith is our willingness to face the fear of what might happen, to trust that, whatever happens, we can cope with it, learn from it, pull things together and move on. We cannot face everything all at once, but we can break it down into small steps, and deal with it bit by bit. Faith is learning to relax – let go – trust the creative process. God the Creator is helping us turn from fear towards faith; starting in small ways; working step by step, as we realize: I can do this. I can do this well. I can choose life. I can move forward. Whatever happens, I can handle it, I will be given help, I am never alone.

Faith says: Whatever happens, I know the way to the Source of life. I have the key to God's treasury. I know that God's resources are infinite, and that they are available to me. I only have to imagine them, pay attention to them, give thanks for them, and trust that God has given them. What I have is enough for this moment. The unknown I entrust to God. All I love is safe in God's keeping. I can take the step before me. The future is not yet my concern.

Question: How is my enjoyment of life undermined by negative emotions such as anxiety? What 'resource' would I like to receive from God's treasury?

Reflection: Isaiah 43.1–7. Do not be afraid . . . You are precious in my eyes . . . I love you.

> Relax, surrender,
> flow,
> let go, have faith,
> sustain my trust.
> It sounds impossible,
> it sounds unlikely,
> it sounds unlike me.
>
> Relax, surrender,
> flow,
> let go, have faith,
> and put my trust
> in what I can do,
> in what they can do,
> in all you can do.
>
> Relax, surrender,
> flow,
> let go, have faith,
> invest my trust
> like a seed in good soil,
> letting the pulse
> of a life
> I cannot see
> lead me onwards
> into light.

The anti-feast

The more we 'imagine abundance', and the more we make it real, the more we discover that fear is our enemy; indeed, that fear is our only enemy. For faith asserts that abundant life is available to all, here and now; while fear, in all its many and varied manifestations, resists even the possibility that this is so. For the fearful, that is not the way the world works. Life just isn't like that. There is not enough to go around. Everyone is only out for what they can grab, and if anyone is going to get left out, it will be me.

This is why the gospel of abundance will always be opposed, and why Mark's account of Jesus' mission is overshadowed by adversity from the outset. In Jesus' home town, his relatives and neighbours resist his message because they know him – or, rather, they think they do – and they cannot understand how he has acquired his ideas, his wisdom and his authority. 'Where did this man get all this?' they ask one another (6.1–6). In other words: If he has been able to acquire all this, why haven't I?

We can feel that the possibility of abundant life is too good to be true: that if it is available at all, it will be given to those who are better or stronger or holier; that if there is anything good going, it will all be gone before we get to it. We can feel that 'It cannot be for me' or 'It won't be good for me' or 'It will never last'. So we resist even the thought of it, because we dread the disappointment of not being good enough to get some; of seeing others enjoying themselves while we are shut out. This is the kind of thinking which leads us to bite the hand that feeds us. Jesus' friends, relatives and neighbours are so wary, so unwilling to be convinced, that there is little he can do to help them.

Nevertheless, he sets off around the villages, teaching, and sends out the Twelve, in pairs, to do the same. Their mission brings his name to the attention of Herod, an ominous development, as this is the man who arrested John the Baptist and ordered his execution (6.14–29). Mark gives us this story in flashback, but by sandwiching it between the departure of the apostles and their return, he shows us how the gospel of abundant life challenges those who exercise power in a manner that is corrupt. Despots secure their position by controlling valuable resources and distributing the benefits amongst their cronies. They fuel the appetites of those around them and keep them in a perpetual state of fear. Naturally, therefore, they oppose the claim that people can enjoy fullness of life without needing to be afraid.

Although Mark does not describe Herod's banquet, we can envisage a scene of lavish, royal hospitality: beautiful surroundings, sumptuous furnishings, luscious food, ample wine, fabulous entertainment. It is an opportunity for Herod to assert his dominance by displaying the various kinds of abundance he can command and distributing largesse to whomsoever he chooses. Those present are his courtiers, officers and the leaders of Galilee, those who derive their power and wealth from being close, useful or necessary to the king.

Like other despots, before and since, Herod has taken what he wants, even if it already belongs to someone else: in this case, he has acquired Herodias, the wife of his brother, Philip. Any power she possesses is threatened by John's public criticisms, so although Herod is protecting John, she seizes the opportunity to have the prophet killed. Herod's offer to the daughter whose dancing has pleased him – anything she wants, up to half his kingdom – is the stuff of legend; a drunken boast; not a promise that any sober ruler would have made, nor that any serious person would expect him to keep. But it is easy enough to imagine that he offered the girl a present, and that she referred the matter to Herodias, who knew exactly what she wanted. And that once Herodias had stated her terms, the king felt obliged to meet them. With his power resting on his ability – and willingness – to give largesse to his followers, he cannot afford to be seen to withhold a gift, even of this kind.

It is not surprising that Herod's agents are found amongst the enemies of Jesus (3.6; 8.15;12.13), for in many ways, the 'feast' of Herod is the exact opposite of the feast of the kingdom which Jesus creates by feeding the multitude. If Jesus is in such demand that he and his disciples do not even have time to eat (6.31), it is, in part, because those who control the abundance of the land are grabbing it, hoarding it, wasting it and spending it solely on themselves, leaving so many starving for bread, wholeness and hope. In this context, the feast of the kingdom represents a radical challenge to the economic and political structures of society. But it confronts them, not by prescribing an alternative means of organizing the resources of the community, but by attacking the fear of people trapped, oppressed and exploited by the system.

Mark does not portray Jesus as a political activist in our terms, but he does show us that Jesus' teaching carries economic and political implications which are nothing short of revolutionary. If people become fired with a vision of God-given abundance, and if they take to heart the message that God is empowering them to enjoy this abundant life, then all that prevents them from claiming it is their fear of the powers that be. It is their fear of the forces ranged against them and the consequences of defiance that prevents them 'imagining abundance' and thinking creatively as to how they might attain it. But if that fear is weakened or removed, then anything becomes possible.

So the gospel is a threat to any corrupt or despotic form of organization because it reduces peoples' fear, enables them to imagine a more benevolent alternative, and empowers them to act as if it is true. In doing so, they start to make it real. The change from fear to faith begins in hidden ways, like a seed germinating in the earth. It grows slowly at first, in a sequence of small steps; each one a tiny change to how we see and think and feel; but gradually altering our approach to situations and our attitude towards other people. At the same time, these changes increase the energy we have available to think and act creatively. They influence both our desire to respond and our ability to do so in a positive, imaginative manner. One small step leads to another, and soon we are considering, not only the task which lies before us and the resources we have to work with, but what kind of process we are involved in and whether it is likely to generate a plenty that can be shared. We begin to look beyond 'What are we doing?' or even, 'What will this achieve?' to ask, 'Where will this lead us?'

Question: How does the feast of the kingdom challenge the way I gain, save and use my money and other material goods?

Reflection: Isaiah 42.1–9. The gentle strength of the Spirit gives the servant of God the faith to create justice.

> Changing the world
> one step at a time,
> we discover
> a road that many
> are travelling;
> shaped by those
> who have left their marks
> to be our signs.
>
> Changing the world
> one link at a time,
> we discover
> how we are connected
> with ourselves,
> with others,
> with the earth
> beneath our feet,
> and the issues which jostle
> for our attention,
> always.
>
> Changing the world
> one choice at a time,
> we discover
> that behind the connections
> are people;
> and powering the issues
> are stories
> which travel with us;
> our companions
> on the way.

Changing the world
one day at a time,
we discover
how to tell the story afresh,
plot ourselves in the action,
and imagine an ending
where the treasure
is found
and the land
renewed.

Looking for a sign

It is not hard to see why the Herodians oppose Jesus, but why are his fellow-teachers so hostile to him? What is it about the message of abundant life which antagonizes the spiritual leaders of his day, those whom Mark describes, variously, as the scribes, Pharisees, chief priests and elders? It seems likely that they share with him a vision of God's infinite grace and a longing to see Israel renewed by the richness of life God has promised. As they believe this will only occur through careful attention to God's word, they see themselves as faithful shepherds of the flock, guardians and interpreters of God's instruction, and responsible for the ultimate safety and welfare of the nation. To this end, they study the scriptures; teach the young; advise on points of law, tradition and custom; and take a lead in community life through the local synagogues.

However, it may be that their faithfulness to the God of Moses and their pastoral care for the people makes them too aware of all that has been lost as their land has been plundered by one empire after another. They see the anguish of widows, orphans and the sick: all those left hungry, grieving, destitute and desolate. They fear that any conflict with the powers that be can only make the situation far worse. If so, their opposition springs from this fear. They are asking: What does the gospel mean for the communities we serve? For the people as a whole? Is it really 'good news'? Is it worth the risk of conflict? It is because they are not convinced on this point that some of them need a sign. They need to see that God is with this movement before they give it their support.

Essentially, they disagree with Jesus on the potential of the present moment: what God is asking of us; what it is possible for us to be, do, achieve and become, here and now. They see the time as a season for fasting rather than feasting (2.18–20), in which the people must prepare for God's intervention by adhering more strictly to the law, which is why they do not understand Jesus' willingness to eat with tax-collectors and sinners (2.15–17), still less his attitude to the Sabbath (2.23 – 3.6). They believe in God's abundance, and ought to possess it, but their fear does not allow them to claim it, so they 'have nothing' (4.25). Not only have they lost sight of the Feast to which everyone is invited, but their fear does not even allow them to enjoy what they have, with the result that 'even what they have will be taken away'. And this affects their judgement: Jesus accuses them of interpreting the 'tradition of the elders' in a manner which denies God's life-giving intentions (7.1–13).

Consequently, the divergence between Jesus and his fellow-teachers is like the difference between a piece of new material, which has never been washed, and an old, well-worn cloak which has been washed, stretched and shrunk many times over. The former cannot be used to patch the latter, because they will tear apart (2.21–22), ruining both. Similarly, new wine cannot be put into an old wineskin.

It is important that we notice this parable, because Jesus is not necessarily saying that the new wine is better than the old. As I understand it, old wine often tastes much better than the raw, effervescent stuff. No, his point seems to be that two things which are so very different cannot be mixed without turmoil, conflict and loss. Some things have to be kept separate, for their own good.

In other words, the fact that Jesus argues with his fellow-teachers and criticizes them does not mean that he is condemning them, or the law. On the contrary, as I have tried to indicate though the biblical passages suggested for further study, the gospel of abundant life is rooted in the Hebrew scriptures. What disturbs Jesus is that so many of his fellow-teachers, pastors and leaders cannot see this. Their vision is limited by fear, which pervades – and therefore distorts – their whole attitude, causing them to interpret the tradition in a manner which 'makes void the word of God' (7.13). Jesus is concerned that those who ought to be heartening the people through their teaching are failing to do so. Worse, they are using God's word in a way which diminishes and discourages others. It is this attitude which grieves him: he is not damning the teachers themselves.

Following the feeding of the four thousand (8.1–10), some Pharisees approach Jesus, asking him for a sign from heaven. Jesus sighs deeply in his spirit – perhaps a suggestion that we are to see this altercation as summing up and symbolizing the whole of his fraught relationship with his fellow-teachers. He refuses: 'Why does this generation ask for a sign? Truly, I tell you, no sign will be given to this generation' (8.11–13). He walks away.

Crossing the lake in the boat with his disciples, he warns them, 'Watch out – beware of the yeast of the Pharisees and the yeast of Herod.' The disciples are puzzled, thinking that he is talking about bread, and perhaps criticizing them for their lack of forethought, because, once again, they have little to hand – only a single loaf. At which point, Jesus becomes exasperated. Don't they get it, even now? Haven't they been watching and listening? Haven't they thought about anything they've seen and heard? 'When I broke the five loaves for the five thousand, how many baskets full of broken pieces did you collect?' he asks them. 'Twelve,' they reply. And when he fed the four thousand? Seven. Well then.

No, this is not about how much bread they have in their hands. Nor is it about how much they have left over when everyone has eaten. Not as such. What Jesus wants them to see is the astonishing process of growth. Five loaves and two fish fed 5,000 people, with 12 baskets left over. Seven loaves and a few small fish fed 4,000 people, with seven baskets left over. It is the difference that he wants them to remember: the infinite resources which lie behind it; the amazing grace which inspires it, the astounding process which generates it, the awesome potential it unlocks. See what God makes possible; look at what can be achieved.

The disciples are focusing on their poverty and weakness in the face of all that needs to be done: on the fact that they are hungry and there is so little food to be had. But hasn't Jesus shown them, again and again, that what we have in our hands does not matter: what matters is what we do with it? And then there are those guardians of the tradition, and shepherds of the people, who are so fearful of taking a risk that they demand a sign from heaven before they will believe. Hasn't Jesus demonstrated that, by applying the principles in the Scriptures, it is possible to feed the multitude?

Why are people unable to see what is before their very eyes? How can he give them a sign from heaven when they are unable to see what they have in their hands?

Question: Is there any context in which I am looking for a sign before I commit myself to a path of creative change? Does my concern for the welfare of others help me to 'imagine abundance' for them – or hinder me in doing so?

Reflection: Joel 2.21–29. A visionary spirit crowns the renewal of the land.

> Spiritual disciplines are a way
> of training ourselves
> to believe.
> There are no short-cuts.
> We grow in faith
> as we live by faith.
> Example. Experiment. Practice.

Learning how we see things,
asking the awkward questions
of ourselves,
examining our prejudices,
reflecting on our assumptions.
It is as we imagine abundance
for ourselves
that we learn to see
how life can be different
for others.
It is as we reshape our responses
with mercy, understanding, love,
that we let go, let God,
trust.
When we feel the potential
of that change, then we see
how we can make a difference.
As we convert the way we see
 – and think about –
what we are doing,
why we are doing it,
how we go about it,
we discover our mission,
not in our actions,
but in the trust
which turns them
into healing fire.

The power of the mustard seed

At what stage did it become clear to Jesus, the disciples and the crowd that the process was working; that the five loaves and two fish would be enough to feed them all? Where did the extra food come from, anyway?

We are not given the answer to any of these questions, so the precise nature of the miracle remains a mystery. And that is probably the point: Mark is less interested in what happened than in the fact that something happened; that something always happens whenever Jesus follows the 'way'. The fact that we have two very similar feeding narratives suggests that Jesus fed crowds of needy people more than once. If so, it is likely that the meal was provided by a different means each time. In one sense, it hardly matters: the marvel is that the food arrives at all. To someone who is seriously hungry, and who is stuck in a barren environment, the miracle is being filled.

That is the point, that they all ate and were filled: that at the end of the process, there was enough to go around; indeed more, far more than enough. There were baskets of broken pieces left over. Who ate the crumbs? Jesus? The disciples? It does not matter. What we are intended to see is the abundance: the fact that there was a vast amount left over. The numbers are no doubt significant. Twelve suggests that the feast of the kingdom will feed all 12 tribes of Israel: while seven may point to the 'seven days' of creation which culminate in the feast of the Sabbath; the implication being that the whole created order shares in God's abundant life.

Mark wants us to see the *process* that made the miracle. He wants us to 'understand about the loaves' because this is the way of faith we use to move from where we are to where we want to be. He is saying to us: understand what Jesus does with the loaves and how he goes about it – because this is how you 'walk on water'.

Jesus' action with the loaves was nothing new. He was simply demonstrating the way he faced every situation, whatever the circumstances. This was the 'way' he was teaching the disciples, and which they had practised during their first independent mission. But what made the feast in the wilderness different was the sheer size of the crowd and the scale of their need. Daunted and dazed by this, and only too aware of their own hunger, the disciples were thrown into confusion and doubt. They failed to recognize the similarities between this situation and those they had already faced successfully. Feeling utterly out of their depth, they had become more and more afraid, and this fear had rendered them unable to offer the gospel.

In feeding the five thousand, Jesus shows us how he makes the gospel real, no matter how large the task. This story is not about one event, but his whole ministry, his life – and his Passion too. The 'way' he applies here, he applied everywhere, all the time: to feed, to heal, to free people, to face his own end. What he shows us is the creative process which allows us to be creative, generous, compassionate, life-giving, even in the most adverse circumstances. What he shows us, as he goes before us, is the path to salvation. Always. Everywhere. For everyone.

The feeding of the five thousand is Jesus' master class in collaborating with the Holy Spirit in the task of generating abundant life. Seen under a microscope, as it were, the process dissolves into a sequence of many small actions, none of which is 'enough' in any sense, and many of which are purely symbolic, apparently meaningless, gestures. But a process is larger than any one action: indeed, it is larger than the sum of all the actions combined. It generates a dynamic – a form of life, energy, power – which causes something to happen, or rather, it causes many things to happen, in succession, across many dimensions, all at once. And it is the total effect of all these tiny events, alterations and realignments which generates 'enough'.

Years ago, someone gave us a 'friendship cake'. This was a yeast-based culture which sat in a bowl in the fridge, and which we had to stir every day and feed occasionally. The culture grew rapidly to fill the bowl, and after a few days we had enough to divide the mixture into three portions. One portion was mixed with other ingredients and baked to make a large, tasty cake. A second portion remained in the bowl in the fridge and continued growing. The third portion was passed on to a friend.

At the time we received the cake, my husband David and I were living in the college where David was training as a Methodist presbyter. We had only been married about 18 months and did not have any children. When we baked our first cake, we liked it very much, but long before we had eaten it up, the culture had produced enough mixture for a second one. Meanwhile, the culture in the fridge grew so quickly that when we went away for a couple of days, the friend who looked after our flat found the cake overflowing the bowl, leaking out of the fridge and onto the kitchen floor. Although there were about 60 students in the college community, most of whom were married and many of whom had children, we soon ran out of friends to whom we could give our surplus portion.

It is this amazing capacity for growth which Mark wants us to see. This is a process which can start from small beginnings and work – sometimes with astonishing speed – to generate an abundance. And, rather like the 'friendship cake', the products of this process can be applied in various ways.

Realization

In the first instance, the process realizes the kingdom in a form appropriate to the need. It earths the vision of abundant life by making the feast personal, practical, specific, real. This is the part of the yeast culture that we bake into a cake and enjoy. There is little point in having a vision of abundance unless the blessing is given specific form and benefits those who share it. Unless it is 'fixed' in this way, it will gradually fade until it is only a fantasy, a form of escapism or a vague, unrealized hope. If the vision is realized – even if it can only be realized in part – then it lives on as an experience, a memory, an example, a story, an inspiration. It remains alive because it remains capable of conveying life to someone else, somewhere else.

Reinforcement and Reinvestment

Secondly, the process reinforces all that the disciples knew already, and which they would have to keep on learning until practising the 'way' came naturally to them. Conversion is a lifelong process of working out how to become more faithful, more trusting, more true as disciples of Jesus and witnesses to his 'way'. We are part of his 'school of faith'. We never stop being disciples. However far we travel, we are always beginning again.

The 'way' is a process of continual reinforcement and reinvestment. We remind ourselves of the vision which calls and resources us. We refer back to it at regular intervals to reorient ourselves, stay on course, and prepare for what comes next.

We keep learning how to receive what is given, how to give thanks, how to act as if the vision is true, and how to persevere. We keep developing our vision and applying the strategy to different circumstances. Each step grows out of the ones before, but at the same time reinforces them. Each step releases energy which we can use, and also reinvest in the process. God invests faith in us; we invest faith in ourselves, in one another, in all that God is doing with us.

In some situations, we have to repeat the cycle again and again, each time starting from a slightly different point. The 'way' is a spiral which returns us to familiar ground, but at a fresh height (or greater depth). Practising the path reinforces our course, enhancing all that is new and life-giving, all that is creative. This is the part of the yeast culture which stays in the fridge. We feed it a little, and it feeds us a lot. It is the 'starter' for each new cycle of growth.

The Ripple Effect

From the beginning, the process generates more than the energy it requires to keep going. The life within it increases rapidly, and as it does so, the impact of the process expands, rippling outwards, from person to person, situation to situation, context to context. We are multi-dimensional beings, immersed in a rich web of relationships, interacting with a multi-faceted culture set in a complex global society. So the effect is not like knocking down a single row of dominoes, where each event causes another event next door. No, it is as if the falling of a single tile sets off a chain reaction in every conceivable direction, all at once, so that events radiate outwards, not only around the surface of a sphere but through the heart of it as well.

This is the part of the 'friendship cake' we give away, and which we keep on giving away, because the bowl is generating far, far more than we can ever eat. If every cup of mixture we give away is nurtured, then it, too, becomes a source of life which feeds our friends, and which they, too, begin to give away. In this manner, the friendship cake spreads around the world.

The 'way' of Jesus is a means of magnifying small investments so that they become sufficient, regardless of the scale of the task. It is not only a means of generating growth, but a means of bridging the gap between what I have and what will meet the need. It is the process which allows the tiny mustard seed to grow until it can shelter a flock of birds (4.30–32).

Question: What is the 'bowl in my fridge' which grows food – to eat, to reinvest, to share? How do I 'stir' the mixture in the bowl each day? How do I feed it? How does it feed me?

Reflection: 1 Kings 17.8–24. Food in the midst of famine.

Abundance begins here:
whoever we are, wherever we are,
with whatever we have been given.

Abundance begins here:
this is where God has chosen to feed us,
and through us, to feed those others
who clamour at our door, our window,
our gate.

Abundance begins here:
for Jesus, the grace of God
is not far off.
It is already at hand.
It is always present.

Abundance begins here:
not a promise pushed into the future,
waiting for a change in the weather,
an improvement in our circumstances,
or the outcome of a review.
It does not depend on the nature of our environment,
or the enthusiasm of our people
or the scale of the resources available to us.
Nor does it hinge on us getting it right,
or even on me getting it right.

Abundance begins here.
Jesus tells us that we do not need
anything more, or anything new,

or anything else.
We already know
all we need to know;
we already hold
all we need to begin.

Because
God is here,
now,
with us,
as we are,
loving us:
abundance begins here.

Always Beginning Again

Knowing how we are fed by God,
that God's resources are infinite,
and that we can draw whatever we need
to face the demands of the journey,
we move out
and move on;
travelling the hard road,
travelling light,
light-hearted, care-free, buoyant;
re-presenting the fluid, overflowing,
renewing Spirit:
God's life,
as Jesus shows us,
as he has taught us,
sowing grain in every kind of soil,
watering seeds wherever we find them,
because there is always more.

O God of the Journey,
guide us to the place where you wait for us,
holding our treasure:
your dream for us alone.

O Jesus our Companion,
be born in our hearts and in our souls,
loving us into freedom:
your dream for us fulfilled.

O Spirit of adventure,
come with us as we take
your path through the wilderness,
seeking abundant life
for ourselves, for our children,
for one another, for the world:
your dream for all people,
forever.

Notes

Chapter 1: A Way to Feed the Multitude
1. Thomas Toke Lynch also wrote of this connection in his hymn, 'My faith, it is an oaken staff', *Hymns & Psalms* no. 682, Methodist Publishing House, 1983.

Chapter 2: The Prospect of a Feast
1. The phrase 'The kingdom comes from the future' is not mine, but I cannot remember where I have read it or heard it. Any suggestions welcome.
2. I owe this thought to Henri Nouwen, who wrote of Jesus' understanding of God's love for him, received at his baptism, as being the 'core experience' of his life and of his identity. Nouwen's ideas on this are quoted in Henri Nouwen, The *Only Necessary Thing: Living a Prayerful Life,* compiled and edited by Wendy Wilson Greer, Darton, Longman & Todd, 2000, p. 67.
3. Charles Wesley, 'Thy ceaseless, unexhausted love' *Hymns & Psalms* no. 48, Methodist Publishing House, 1983.

Chapter 3: Meeting the Multitude
1. See, for example: Psalms 23; 77.16–20; 79.13; 80.1–2; 95.6–7; 100.3; Isaiah 40.11; Ezekiel 34.

Chapter 4: Receiving the Gift
1. This meditation originally appeared under the title 'Threshold', in my self-published booklet, *The Light Beyond the Wall: Poems from praying in dark places*, in 1991.

Chapter 5: The Art of Abundance
1. 'The Sunday Service' from *The Methodist Service Book*, Methodist Publishing House, 1975.
2. T.S. Eliot, 'Burnt Norton', *Four Quartets*, Faber & Faber, 1944, lines 42–43.
3. Michel Quoist, *Prayers of Life*, Gill & Macmillan Ltd, 1963, page 5. The phrase relates specifically to the importance of being alert to the Passion of Christ in the suffering of others, but the idea of paying close attention to all of life permeates Quoist's work. He started me thinking about what it means to pay attention to the present moment.

Chapter 7: The School of Faith
1. The description of prayer as 'letting the sap rise' comes from the writing and preaching of the Revd Donald Eadie.
2. For an excellent self-help book on facing our fear in all sorts of situations, see Susan Jeffers, *Feel the Fear and Do It Anyway: How to turn your fear and indecision into confidence and action*, Arrow Books, 1991. Jeffers writes in a

breezy, accessible style and her practical exercises work. I know, because I used several of them to gather the courage to write this book and to keep writing it until it was complete. I also recommend Julia Cameron, *The Artist's Way: A Course in Discovering and Recovering your Creative Self*, Pan Macmillan Ltd, 1995. Cameron's exercises are more time-consuming, but they repay the investment, and are particularly useful for anyone finding their way through self-doubt to a greater creativity.